# dedication

It's with sincere gratitude that I thank Sara Domville, Nancy Soriano, Christine Doyle and Tonia Davenport for the opportunity to spend the last year contentedly wrapped in stitches.

As always, I'm grateful to my family who put up with a dining room filled with fabric and a few fiber-laced meals. Sending a big smooch to my husband Jon, who is unfailing in his support of my crafty pursuits.

# acknowledgements

I love a good excuse to buy fabric; even better than the spending spree is when goodies arrive free of charge. Just as the design work for this book got underway, my sister Sasha, a talented art director, generously presented me with her gorgeous fabric stash. Carefully purchased by design and color, it was ready and waiting for each new project. Christi Henke at National Nonwovens made sure that I had every color and variety of their amazing felt at my fingertips.

Fuzzy thanks to LK Success for sending me a wonderful selection of felt flowers and beads.

My editor, Julie Hollyday, took my mishmash of instructions, copy, files, pages of illustration and boxes full of projects and turned them into the book you hold in your hands. The photographic, graphic and photo stylings of Ric Deliantoni, Ronson Slagle, Lauren Emmerling and Jan Nickum, respectively, brought the whimsical projects to a whole new level of cuteness.

# about the author

Heidi Boyd is the author of a dozen craft books with North Light Books. Her goal is to make sophisticated design approachable and easy for all. She fell in love with all things crafty when she was a child and is pleased as punch that she's found a way to keep creating as a grown-up.

She first sat down at a sewing machine during a summer high school class in Beaconsfield, Quebec, Canada. Many years later she completed a fine art degree at University of New Hampshire. She got her start in professional crafting as a contributor to *Better Homes and Gardens* books and magazines. Currently, she regularly sews up new creations for *Stitch* magazine.

Heidi, her husband Jon, their three children and their new puppy, Otto, enjoy the natural beauty of their home in the Maine woods.

Stop by her blog heidiboyd.blogspot.com for more crafty ideas.

# table of contents

# stitched whimsy

## Playful projects in felt & fabric

## Heidi Boyd

**NORTH LIGHT BOOKS**

CINCINNATI, OHIO

media   www.fwmedia.com

15  14  13  12  11    5  4  3  2  1

DISTRIBUTED IN CANADA BY FRASER DIRECT
100 Armstrong Avenue
Georgetown, ON, Canada  L7G 5S4
Tel: (905) 877-4411

DISTRIBUTED IN THE U.K. AND EUROPE BY F&W MEDIA INTERNATIONAL
Brunel House, Newton Abbot, Devon, TQ12 4PU, England
Tel: (+44) 1626 323200, Fax: (+44) 1626 323319
Email: enquiries@fwmedia.com

DISTRIBUTED IN AUSTRALIA BY CAPRICORN LINK
P.O. Box 704, S. Windsor NSW, 2756 Australia
Tel: (02) 4577-3555

SRN: YO236
ISBN-13: 978-1-4403-0913-7

edited by Julie Hollyday
designed by Ronson Slagle
production coordinated by Greg Nock
photography by Ric Deliantoni
photo styling by Lauren Emmerling
cover styling by Jan Nickum
illustrations by Heidi Boyd

## metric conversion chart

| to convert | to | multiply by |
| --- | --- | --- |
| inches | centimeters | 2.54 |
| centimeters | inches | 0.4 |
| feet | centimeters | 30.5 |
| centimeters | feet | 0.03 |
| yards | meters | 0.9 |
| meters | yards | 1.1 |

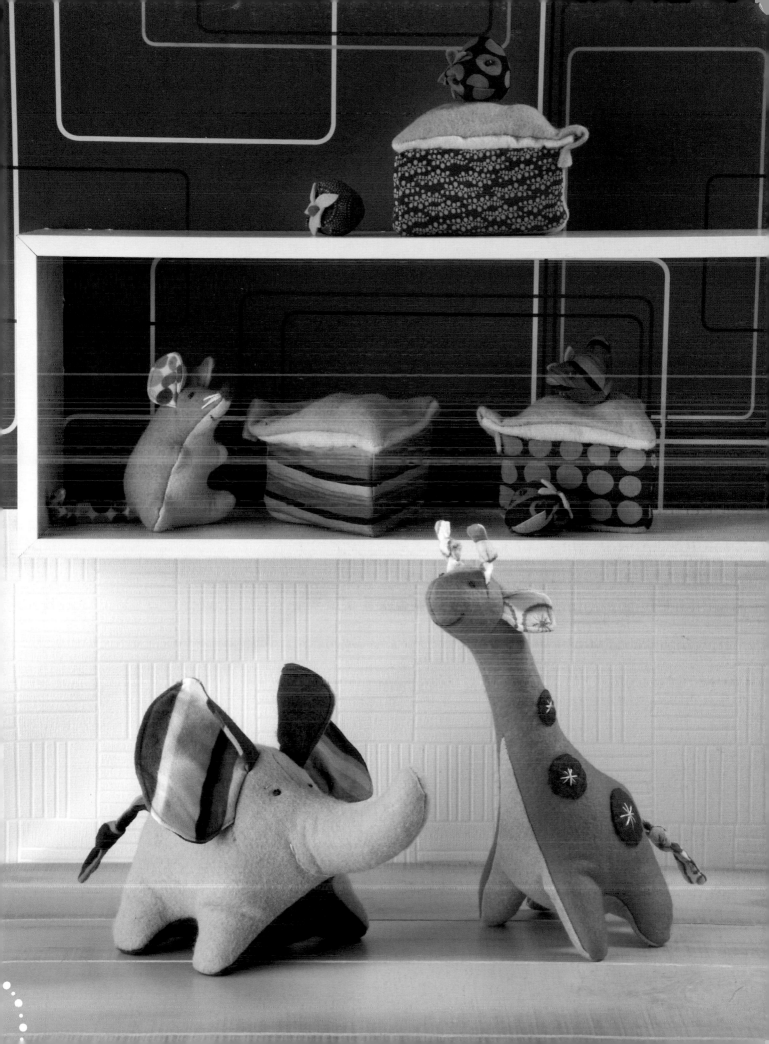

# introduction

**When I was a child,** I designed and hand stitched stuffed animals for my little brothers. I'm not sure if they appreciated my handmade gifts, but I keenly remember how much I enjoyed making them. I never stopped creating, and years of professional crafting have familiarized me with an astounding variety of crafting materials. This book offered the unique opportunity to integrate my love of sewing with beading, needle felting and mixed-media crafting. It was an absolute joy to create, and I sincerely hope it brings you many happy hours of stitching.

Prepare yourself for an overload of cuteness. Sewing up the projects in this book is guaranteed to put a smile on your face. I have as much fun stitching up these designs as I do gifting them and selling them at craft fairs. When greeted with vibrant colors in fun designs, people can't help but chuckle and grin. They instinctively reach out to touch the soft fabric pairings. The small size and sweet facial expressions of softies like the *Happy Hedgehogs* on page 68 beg to be held, hugged and loved.

Non-traditional fabric combinations are the key to the easy construction and textural appeal of these whimsical designs. Gorgeous prints zing with pattern and color while fleece and felt add softness. Both fleece and felt have the advantage of no-fray edges, eliminating sewing steps. Wool felt also is the superstar of many of the creations; it's available in a stunning array of colors and coordinates with any fabric selection. Its heft gives structure to the projects and also allows you to needle felt wool roving directly into the fiber. Almost every project needs less than a yard of fabric. The "perfect" fabric makes all the difference. Enjoy the process and take time to choose what will work best for each project.

Sewing up any of the designs is quick and simple, making the book perfect for beginning sewers as well. I machine stitched almost everything with the simple straight-stitched seams. Basic embroidery stitches are used to add faces and encircle appliquéd felt. Beauty is in the details, and I've included instructions and tips to help you embellish your whimsical creations with felt flowers, beads, buttons and sequins.

Whether you choose to cook up slices of bright cherry pie or create sleepy owls with layered flower eyes, your efforts are sure to spread whimsical fun to your family and friends.

# materials

Most of the projects in this book require small amounts of materials so you'll be able to get started making cute creations with minimal expense. If you're already a sewer, you'll need to add just a few unique supplies—most likely a selection of quality wool felt, wool roving and new embellishments. I haven't met a crafter who isn't excited about new supplies, so go out and have fun. I've included some suggestions of where to locate items.

## Wool Felts

Wool felt brings structure and substance to the designs in this book. Please don't confuse it with its distant acrylic cousins. Wool felt is incredibly pleasing to the touch. It has some stretch but doesn't become distorted like acrylic felts.

Wool felt can't be machine washed; use a lint brush to remove stray fibers and a damp cloth to clean your creations.

National Nonwovens provided all the felt that is used in the book. They make a fabulous product that is available in an astounding array of colors.

Read through the following information to familiarize yourself with the varieties of wool contents and sources that are called out in the materials list of each project.

### 35% Wool Felt

Like it stipulates, this is a nonwoven felt that has a 35% wool content. This is the felt of choice for most of the projects in the book. It has some heft that strengthens and gives structure to the designs, but it is easy to cut and stitch.

### 100% Wool Felt

A wonderfully rich nonwoven fiber, 100% wool fiber's greatest asset is that you can noodle felt directly into this fiber. For this reason I intentionally incorporated it into some of the softie faces. It's possible to substitute felted sweater fabrics, but it usually doesn't have the smooth surface of this product. Because of the expense, it is used in small areas—a little bit can go a long way.

### XoticFelt

This is made with bamboo fibers. It is a great, environmentally friendly fabric. It's lighter weight than the 35% wool felt, and I often choose it for its bright colors.

### Plush Felt

This type of felt has the appearance of polyester fur without the heavy knit base. Plush felt is made with recycled plastic bottles. The lightweight felt base makes it easy to cut and stitch; I'd recommend it for children's sewing projects.

### Stiffened Felt

Sold in craft stores, this rigid felt is stiffened with starch. It's great for small accents, like bird beaks, where its rigidity is an asset.

### Felted Recycled Sweaters

You can use felted sweaters to make all kinds of softie creations. The material is bulky and can be challenging for some sewing machines. I used it sparingly in this book in places where designs needed extra texture and bulk.

You can easily felt 100% wool sweaters in your washing machine. Wash them with warm water and soap, then machine dry. The sweaters should shrink and make a thick, bulky fabric that won't fray.

## Fabrics

Fabrics are the flashy stars of this book. The splash of color and pattern makes the other fabrics sing—without them, my designs would lack whimsy. If you're going to take the time to make something by

hand, I can't stress enough how important it is to use the very best fabrics. Almost all the projects in this book use ¼ yard of cotton or less, so even the most expensive fabrics will cost only a few dollars. If you don't have a local fabric store, fire up your computer and shop some of the amazing online sites.

Read on for descriptions of some of the most-used fabrics in the book.

### Printed Cotton Fabric

If you sew or quilt, you probably already have enough scraps in your stash to make all of the projects in this book, but no one needs to know that. Go ahead and treat yourself to a shopping spree.

If you're placing an order, keep in mind: many of the projects, like the *Tabletop Trees* on page 54, *Fanciful Houses* on page 62, *Hilarious Hoots* on page 84 and *Cherry Strawberry Pie* on page 36, use multiple fabrics in the same color family. Also, combine small prints with more open designs, stripes or dots for fun pattern play.

### Flannel

Incredibly soft to the touch, flannel is an excellent choice for baby toys. It's being

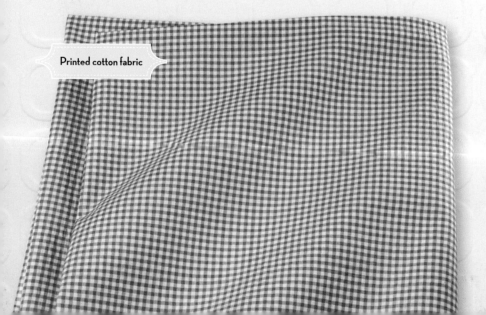

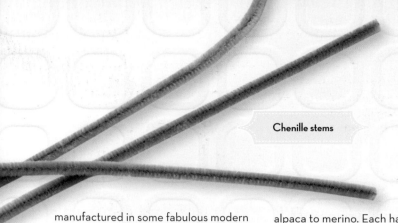

manufactured in some fabulous modern designs for today's hip kids. You only need a little bit, so enjoy splurging on your favorites.

### Corduroy

Often overlooked in softie design, corduroy adds dimension and texture. When I incorporated corduroy into the *Mushroom Pincushion* (page 94), I immediately knew I'd cinched the design. Look for a variety of widths and colors.

## Polyester and Acrylic Blends

Cotton and wool are my favorite fabrics, but there's no denying that acrylic blends have merit and add to the diverse appearance of the projects.

### Plush Fur

This fun fabric comes in a variety of lengths and colors. Plush adds texture and contrast to the smooth felt and cottons. The leopard print that I used in *Happy Hedgehogs* on page 68 makes spines. The best time to find these novelty fabrics is around Halloween.

### Fleece

This snuggly fabric comes in a stunning array of colors, making it easy to coordinate with printed fabrics. It also shares the no-fray advantage of felt.

## Wool Roving

This is sheep fleece that has been washed, carded and dyed but hasn't been spun into yarn. Wool roving can be rolled, shaped with your fingers and then needle felted to hold the shape. Roving comes in a host of different wool varieties from

alpaca to merino. Each has a slightly different texture; experiment with different varieties to find what works best for your budget and your favorite projects. Wool roving is available wherever spinning supplies are sold. It's sometimes available in yarn shops, but if you're having trouble finding it in a local store, you can easily order it online.

### Curly Roving

This wool hasn't been carded and retains its natural curly texture. I used a natural color for the *Gnome Doll*'s beard (page 26) and a dyed color for the *Mermaids and Fairies* hairstyles (page 30).

### Fill Roving

Fill roving are inexpensive mill scraps and are usually white. You can use it as an under layer for bigger needle felt creations. You can wrap it around wire forms to create shape and then use more expensive or prettier merino rovings for the finished outer appearance. I did just that with the creatures from the *Tree Tote With Forest Friends* (page 20).

## Stuffing

There are multiple ways to stuff a whimsical creation. Every project benefits from a different variety of filling. Softness is desirable for a huggable creation whereas rigidity is needed to support some projects.

It's important that any projects stuffed with nontraditional stuffing, such as paper, wire or beans, stay dry. If wet,

these items will lose their stiffness, rust or leach colors into the fabrics.

### Fiberfill

Any soft stuffing can be used to fill your creation. You can select renewable bamboo or polyester, just to name a couple, depending on your purpose and budget. Different brands and price points of fiberfills have different properties. Some may stay in place better and not clump. Do some experimentation to find what works best for you. I use so much stuffing that I take advantage of bulk discounts and sales to keep it on hand.

### Styrofoam

Styrofoam is a great way to stuff and add form and dimension to your stitched creation. Usually sold with the floral supplies in craft stores, it's available in a multitude of shapes and sizes. You can also use a serrated kitchen knife to cut shapes down to size. You can needle felt directly into Styrofoam, which is a great way to quickly add texture to the wool roving that covers it.

### Chenille Stems

Chenille stems, also known as pipe cleaners, are widely available at craft stores. They form the base skeleton of the wool roving creations in this book. They also help strengthen parts of designs that are meant to stand up or be bendable.

### Cardboard

Recycled cereal box cardboard and posterboard are handy items to help add structure to some projects. The trick is to cut the cardboard smaller than the sewn piece so it fits inside. Don't get these wet, as the cardboard will lose its rigidity.

### Paper Pet Bedding

Sold in pet stores to line the bottoms of hamster and gerbil cages, paper bedding has extra weight and helps stabilize projects so they stay right side up. You could easily substitute small dried beans for paper bedding.

# Embellishments

Don't underestimate the importance of finishing touches. The right bead or button can make all the difference to a softie face. Spend the time to find the perfect accents to complete your creation.

### Safety Eyes

As their name states, these eyes are the perfect choice for children's toys. When properly attached, they're almost impossible to pull out. They have two parts: a plastic screw-shaped eye and a metal or plastic washer that slides up the screw to anchor the eye in place.

### Buttons

Buttons are primarily used for eyes, making the two-hole variety the preferred choice. Use a variety of styles and shapes, or showcase the one-of-a-kind buttons in your stash. Shank buttons have the holes behind the button and can easily be substituted for safety eyes when sewing for older children.

### Wood Beads

I like to keep a strand of ¼" (6mm) round wood beads on hand for eyes and noses. They make a great natural pairing with brown and tan felts. Use these for the projects intended for older children and adults.

### Seed and E Beads

Seed beads are small, inexpensive, irregular glass beads that come in a rainbow of colors. They have a narrow opening that requires a small-sized needle. For that reason I primarily use E beads, which are slightly larger and can accommodate a regular sewing needle. Make sure whatever assortment you purchase includes black, which is useful for eyes on small projects.

### Ribbon

Sometimes a simple bow can make all the difference. Take the time to match the fabric in your piece to the ribbon. Bring your projects into the store to have a fun matching session.

### Embroidery Floss

You can never have enough colors of embroidery floss in your sewing basket.

If needed, separate the threads by cutting the strand to the desired length and then pull one thread out at a time while holding the other strands in place. When you have the required number of strands, bring the ends together and string them through the needle. The thickness of embroidery floss requires you to use a larger sized needle.

DMC is my first choice for stitching threads—they have an amazing variety of colors and the smooth floss slides effortlessly through felt and fabric.

### Felt Flowers

Felt flowers are a wonderful way to add pops of color to a design. You can make your own using small scissors and the chosen felt, you could make them using a die cut machine, or you could purchase felt flowers readymade.

I prefer the appearance of die-cut flowers to hand-cut ones, so I invested in a Sizzix BIGkick. It's adept at cutting through multiple layers of felt while producing clean lines.

If you're not interested in investing in a cutting machine, there are many artists who sell precut felt flowers on Etsy.com and Artfire.com. Small felt flowers can also be found with the scrapbooking supplies.

### Felt Buttons

These buttons are widely available in both fabric and craft stores. Use them for closures and embellishments.

### Felt Beads

Felts beads are fun baubles to add to a design. You can roll your own beads out of wool roving or purchase readymade

Ribbon

beads. I outline instructions for making felt beads in my book *Simply Beaded Bliss*—a great way to incorporate matching colors—but I admit that I used purchased beads in this book. Find wool beads in local and online craft stores; find some one-of-a-kind felt beads on Etsy.com.

### Sewing Thread

When stitching will be visible, it's preferable to use a thread that will match and blend with the fabrics. In those cases, I used a good-quality colored thread that wouldn't break while sewing through the bulk. Gutermann was my choice.

For long-lasting projects, I made the unconventional decision to use an off-white machine quilting thread for most of the projects in this book. Its heavier weight easily handles the bulky mix of fabrics. It comes in a large spool; fill up a set of bobbins and be ready to sew your way through a bunch of projects.

# tools

To get started the only tools you really need are a basic sewing machine, scissors, needles and thread. Tools like a rotary cutter and cutting mat make cutting quicker and easier. As your love of sewing grows, add more machinery for quicker production.

## Sewing Machine

No bells and whistles are required to stitch up the designs in this book. I sew on a twenty-year-old Bernette (tiny Bernina) that was a wedding gift. It does have solid metal construction and has no trouble stitching through layers of felt, fleece and plush fur. The most complicated stitch I used was the zigzag.

I can't stress enough how important it is to have your machine serviced, oiled and cleaned. I occasionally have thread tension issues that can only be solved with a service. Use caution sewing around children, and turn off and unplug your machine before leaving your work area.

## Needles

Sewing needles are an essential tool, so make sure you have assorted sizes on hand. If you have trouble threading needles, purchase a needle threader to help with the task. Make the *Tweet Needle Case* (page 106) as one of your first projects so you always have a place to keep your needles.

### Sewing Needles

It's a good idea to purchase an assortment so you'll have what you need on hand. Thicker fabric will need a thicker needle; more delicate fabrics will use thinner ones.

### Sewing Machine Needles

It is good to have a variety of needle sizes. If you're stitching through thick layers, increase the size of your needle to get the job done. Sewing through delicate fabric? A smaller needle size is needed. Be sure to purchase machine needles that are compatible with your sewing machine.

## Crewel Needle

This is my needle of choice for embroidery in this book. It has a wide enough hole to incorporate a full thickness of embroidery thread and a sharp enough point to easily penetrate felt.

## Cutting Tools

A good pair of scissors designated for fabric cutting is a must. You'll find them especially important when you're cutting through heavyweight felt, fleece and plush fur.

### Fabric Scissors

It's handy to have a large pair of scissors for big jobs and a small pair for cutting in and around small spaces. Fiskars Softouch and Mundial FreeStyle are two of my favorite scissors.

### Embroidery Scissors

These tiny scissors have small blades and sharp points. I keep a pair tucked in with my embroidery floss for cutting thread lengths and knots.

### Fabric Pinking Shears

Not to be confused with paper scissors that cut decorative shapes, these heavyweight pinking shears should be used exclusively on fabric to retain their sharp

Sewing needles

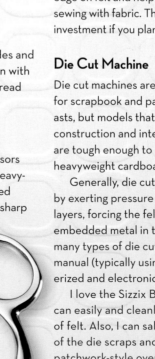

edge. Pinking shears cut a beautiful zigzag edge on felt and help prevent fraying while sewing with fabric. They are a worthwhile investment if you plan to continue sewing.

## Die Cut Machine

Die cut machines are produced primarily for scrapbook and paper craft enthusiasts, but models that boast heavy-duty construction and interchangeable dies are tough enough to cut through felts and heavyweight cardboards.

Generally, die cut machines work by exerting pressure between two rigid layers, forcing the felt to be cut by the embedded metal in the die. There are many types of die cut machines, including manual (typically using a crank), computerized and electronic styles.

I love the Sizzix BIGkick because it can easily and cleanly cut multiple layers of felt. Also, I can salvage large pieces of the die scraps and reposition them patchwork-style over the die, eliminating much of the waste typical of die cutting.

Fabric scissors

### Circle and Flower Dies

Die designs come and go all the time, creating a great selection and the opportunity to buy some styles on clearance. Some dies have multiple sections intended to create a whole layered piece—use the individual pieces or combine them for the layered effect. Carefully examine die selections to see what designs will work best for your whimsical creations; avoid internal decorative cut lines that will weaken the cut felt.

### Rotary Cutter, Straightedge and Cutting Mat

This threesome works together so people like me can actually cut straight pieces of fabric! A rotary cutter looks like a pizza cutter and has a changeable, retractable blade. Both the cutting mat and the clear straightedge are ruled.

Lay the fabric on the mat, aligning it with one of the ruled lines. Align the straightedge with the mat and use it to guide the rotary cutter across the fabric. With a sharp blade you should be able to cut through multiple layers of fabric easily.

## Needle Felting

Needle felting requires its own unique tools. The start-up investment is minimal as you can get started with a single felting needle and a small amount of wool roving. I love this craft but struggle to keep my attention on the needle so I don't inadvertently poke myself.

### Felting Needles

This needle is typically 3"–4" (7.5cm–10cm) long and features a hooked top. Unlike smooth sewing needles, felting needles have small barbs down their lower half. The barbs are vital: when poked in and out of the roving, they weave the individual fibers together. The hook allows the needle to be stabilized into a handle/tool or gives you something to hold onto if you're using it alone. Felting needles tend to bend and break, so keep a few on hand so you won't have to stop what you're working on if one breaks.

### Needle Felting Tool

This tool is essentially a handle that can be outfitted with three or five needles. It's invaluable for felting large sections of roving quickly and easily. I prefer the Clover three-needle pen-style tool that I used for all the needle-felted projects in this book. They also make a five-needle tool that has a retractable shield to protect your fingers. Both tools unscrew to easily replace broken needles.

### Insulation Board or Felting Pad

You need to needle felt over a surface that you can penetrate the felting needle into while protecting what is underneath.

I've been using pieces of rigid foam insulation left over from a home improvement job. Simply cut a piece down to a comfortable size for your lap and poke away. If one area of the foam becomes worn, move the piece around. Finally, flip the foam over and work on the other side before discarding it.

A brush needle felting pad is an excellent tool if you don't want to throw out foam, but it typically has a smaller working area. Clover manufactures a brush-style felting mat for this purpose.

## Adhesives

For the most part, the projects in this book are stitched together and very little glue is used. Once in a while a dab of glue comes in handy to add a pom-pom to a reindeer's nose, to add a felt bead inside an acorn cap or to anchor the base of a tree to its dowel rod trunk.

I like mini glue guns with low melt sticks. The mini size allows you to easily

control a smaller amount of glue and get into tight areas. After using the glue gun, I always place it on a heat protected surface and out of reach of little hands while it cools—the back of the stove is a good spot.

## Woodworking Tools

A few basic woodworking tools will come in handy if you're intending to make a few of the projects in this book.

### Electric Drill

While any handheld drill will work, I'm least intimidated by the Dremel tool. It fits comfortably in my hand and is ideal for small drilling jobs. I prefer a standard drill outfitted with a ⅛" (3mm) and a ½" (1.5cm) bit. Please use caution whenever operating power tools. Follow all the manufacturer's instructions, work over a protective surface and wear protective eyewear.

### Saw

Use a handsaw or band saw to cut down the length of the dowel rods of the *Tabletop Trees* (page 54).

### Staple Gun

A standard staple gun is used to attach appliquéd fabric to a readymade canvas. Work over a protected surface and keep your fingers clear of the staple area.

## Chalk pencils and marking pens

If freestitching isn't your thing, you can mark stitch lines using chalk pencils or marking pens. When necessary I recommend using disappearing ink fabric markers on the cotton fabrics and chalk pencils on felts. These items are sold in the notions sections of fabric stores. The thermo sensitive ink in Frixion ball point pens (Pilot) disappears after being heated with an iron. It's a popular choice for embroidery and creative stitching. Whichever product you use, test them on scraps before marking. When marking felt, use a light touch to avoid leaving permanent marks or distorting the felt surface.

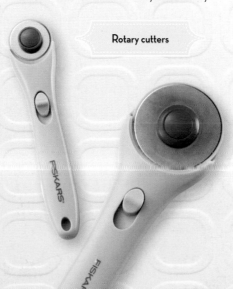

**Rotary cutters**

# getting started

Take a quick moment before you start stitching up cuteness to read through this list of simple techniques and suggestions. They take you through the basic steps involved in stitching up a whimsical creation. I've also included tips to help you machine stitch, stuff and sew on embellishments. Refer to this guide if you have trouble following the more abbreviated individual project directions.

## General Rules for Templates, Patterns and Fabric

After you've selected your fabrics, it's time to cut those beauties into the right size pieces.

### Preparing the Pattern

Locate the patterns for your project on pages 109–126. Follow the directions to enlarge them on a photocopier. Cut the paper pattern pieces out and carefully arrange them over the specified fabrics.

### Cutting the Fabric

Leave at least ¼" (6mm) of fabric around each pattern piece for the seam allowance, unless otherwise noted, and pin the paper pattern to the fabric. Use fabric scissors to cut out the pattern piece; be sure to cut ¼" (6mm) from the paper edge. Without the seam allowance, your finished piece will be very small. Read the project instructions carefully, as some patterns do not require a seam allowance.

### Cutting on the Fold

When the pattern indicates cutting on the fold, align the straight edge of the pattern piece directly against a folded edge of the fabric. Cut the pattern out through both layers of fabric, and you'll end up with a single connected pattern piece. It's quicker to cut multiple pattern pieces out of two layers of folded fabric. This is especially true when cutting out arms and ears; be sure to leave enough room around all the edges for the ¼" (6mm) seam allowance.

### Fabric Preparation

When sewing, prewashing the fabric is typically a must, but because so many of the projects in this book use a combination of non-washable felt and nontraditional stuffing materials, they will never end up in your washing machine. Enjoy being lazy and cut right into that new stiff fabric.

If surface washing (see Whimsy Care on page 16) doesn't cut it for you, feel free to switch up your fabric choices so you can put the whole item in the wash. It is then advisable to prewash the fabrics.

### Ironing

I'm not a fan of ironing, but sometimes it can't be avoided. Wrinkly fabric needs to be tamed before it can be properly cut and sewn. Be careful when ironing wool felt; keep the heat setting turned down. Felt will quickly discolor under extreme heat.

## Sewing Machine Techniques

Nothing fancy here, just some basic techniques to help you machine your way through the stitching process.

### Before You Stitch

Before you start make sure your machine is running in top condition. If you're pulling it out of storage, it will probably need a tune-up and cleaning. It's worth the expense of servicing it instead of cursing your way through a project while it's not working well.

Fill your bobbin and thread your machine with the same thread, then use fabric scraps that match what you're about to stitch and test your seam. Adjust the tension stitch length until you're pleased with the appearance. And don't be afraid to seek help—after all these years, I still pull out my manual to troubleshoot problems.

### Beginning and Ending

Backstitch a ½" (1.5cm) or so at the beginning and end of your seam. This extra step will help prevent the ends of the seam from unraveling. If you're topstitching and the seams will remain visible, skip the backstitch step. In this instance the extra seams aren't attractive.

### Securing Threads

If you backstitch the ends of your seams, it's safe to trim the thread close to the end of the last stitch. If you haven't backstitched, be sure to take the time to tie the ends together. To do this, start by working on the right side of the fabric. Poke the needle down into the point of entry of the last stitch. Thread the top thread through the eye of the needle. Push the needle out the back side of the fabric and knot the top thread to the bottom thread. Trim the excess thread. Repeat the process with the other end of the stitch.

### Turning a Corner

Switching stitching directions is a breeze. Set the needle down into the fabric, lift the presser foot to release the tension on the surrounding fabric. Swivel the fabric to the desired direction. Reset the presser foot and continue stitching. Once you've done this a few times it will be instinctive and you'll be switching directions all the time.

### Free-Form Stitching

Free-form stitching is like drawing lines with your sewing machine. It's the way I stitched the stems in the *Mushroom Canvas* (page 50) and topstitch along patterned fabric. No special attachment foot is necessary; just keep your sewing speed down and slowly move the fabric so the needle makes stitches exactly where you want them. If you reach points like the end of a leaf or the mushroom gills in the *Mushroom Pincushion* (page 94), switch directions by following the Turning a Corner instructions. You can also transfer the stitch lines onto the felt or fabric using a marking pen before stitching.

## Softie Sewing Basics

You've got your fabric and your machine is up and running—let the good times roll.

### Right Sides Together

*Right sides together* means inside out. We sew on the wrong side so the seams are hidden. For this reason you'll find that many of the steps start by asking you to place the right sides of the fabric together. This book features a number of felt and fleece projects that don't require turning the fabric or stitching on the wrong sides; because those fabrics don't fray I intentionally chose to keep the seams visible in some spots.

### Stop and Check Your Seams

Whenever you make a seam it's a good idea to check your work before continuing. Turn the piece over to make sure the seam caught the fabric edges on the other side. You can also turn it right side out and check the inside. This is especially important if you're trapping arms or ears in the seam. If you've missed anything, make a second seam inside from the first and check it again.

### Be Tough: Reinforce

Even if you don't need to correct your first seam, it's a good idea to reinforce your work with a second seam. The second seam is stitched outside of the first seam and helps prevent the fabric edges from fraying. It's especially important to reinforce the seams at joints that might be pulled in loved softies—arms, ears, legs and tails.

### Trim Corners

When you turn your work right side out, extra fabric will add bulk and fill up tight places. It's a good idea to trim away excess fabric, but carefully. Leave a ⅛" (3mm) edge so you don't create a fraying issue. Clip away triangular sections at corners, points, hat tips, ears and tails.

## Go Ahead and Stuff

"Child's play," you say? Don't be so quick to judge. It's not as easy as it looks!

### Small Areas First

Arm yourself with a stuffing stick, which looks like a blunt-ended wooden chopstick. If you can't find one, a knitting needle or the eraser end of a pencil works almost as well. Start by filling the nooks and crannies, like hat points, noses, hands and feet. Next fill the large areas.

### How Much Is Enough?

Let the natural shape of the design guide you. I usually tightly stuff softies, knowing that they will be smooshed and compressed when hugged and loved. Use caution not to overstuff your creation because stuffing can pull at the seams, overstretch the fabric and distort the shape. It's easy to rectify by pulling stuffing out.

## The Finishing Touches

You're almost there, but cuteness requires an adorable face and irresistible embellishments.

### Adding Safety Eyes

Call me crazy, but I like to place the eyes on my softie after the head is stuffed. It's the only time you can place them exactly where you want them. The downside is that you have to fight with stuffing to reach inside and slide the washer backs onto the screw end of the eye. If you're easily frustrated by this kind of process set the eyes before you stitch or before

you stuff. You can test stuff the head first to predict how the fabric will stretch.

The first step is to use embroidery or other small scissors to snip a tiny opening on either side of the head. Push the screw end of the eye into the opening so the plastic eye sits on top. Reach inside the head and thread the backing up onto the screw. You'll need to exert a lot of pressure to slide the backing all the way up so it rests right behind the eye, trapping the fabric between the two plastic pieces.

### Embellishments

The rest of the embellishments are hand stitched in place with a sewing needle and matching sewing thread.

Hiding knots is an easy way to make your project look finished while keeping the embellishments solidly in place. To do this, reach inside an opening to pull the thread up and out of the finished side of the project, leaving the knot hidden on the inside. You can also hide knots in plush fur, under the embellishment or behind an ear.

I like to use multiple stitches to sew on button eyes or felt bead noses to ensure that they won't fall off when kids play with them. I intentionally stitch back and forth inside the head so the eyes get pulled into the center of the head. When you're finished knot the end either inside the head or where you started.

Felt flowers and sequins are a beautiful touch, and I use a bead or button to hold them in place. String the center of the largest flower onto the needle first, then follow with smaller flowers, sequins and a bead or button. Bring the needle back down through the other side of the button and through the sequin and flowers. When you're using only a bead, bring the needle back through the sequin and flowers. The bead will rest on top.

### Closing the Deal

I intentionally leave this step for last. While an opening remains open, you can reach inside to sew on an embellishment or adjust the stuffing.

When you're satisfied with the embellishments, you'll want to securely close the opening. To do this, begin by threading a sewing needle with matching colored thread. Hide your knot inside the piece and tuck the cut fabric ends inside the piece to blend with the machine stitching. Make small stitches that span from one fabric to another. Pull your stitches tight enough to make the stitches invisible but not so tight that the fabric puckers. If possible pass the thread up inside the piece to tie a knot in a hidden location.

The other option is to pass invisible stitches back and forth under the seam until you're sure that the thread is stabilized, knot and then trim the end.

### Whimsy Care

After all your effort, keep the surface of your whimsical creation clean and pretty using the surface washer technique: simply wipe the surface with a dampened cloth and allow it to dry.

If you opted to make the project out of all washable fabrics (see Fabric Preparation on page 14), I strongly recommend placing the items in a garment bag or pillowcase before placing them into the washing machine. This will help protect your creations. Allow them to air dry.

# embroidery stitches

Hand stitching your sewn creations is like signing your work. It brings personality and individuality to your creation. Almost all the embroidery in this book is done with a crewel needle and at least three strands of floss. To make your embroidery pop, use a full strand of contrasting colored floss. Conversely, for subtle embellishments match the floss to your fabric and use fewer strands.

## Blanket Stitch

Traditionally used to finish a cut edge, it strengthens and decorates the fabric.

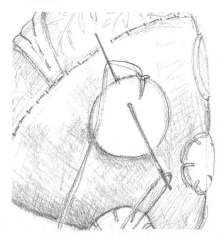

### How to do the blanket stitch

Bring the needle up along the fabric edge. Pierce the needle back into the fabric ¼" (6mm) from the edge. Before pulling the needle all the way out, wrap the thread around the needle tip as it emerges from under the fabric. Start each new stitch ¼" (6mm) away from the last stitch and ¼" (6mm) in from the outside edge. Hook each new stitch to the previous stitch until you've encircled the piece. Link the final stitch to the first stitch along the outside edge and hide your knot under your work.

## Whipstitch

Quickly joins two fabric edges together.

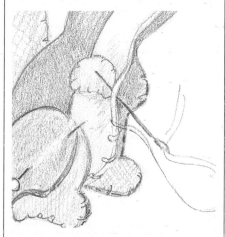

### How to do the whipstitch

Hide your knot between the layers of fabric, then draw the needle through both layers of fabric approximately ⅛" (3mm) from the edge. Wrap the thread over the outside edge and then pierce the needle through both layers of fabric again. If you pull your stitches too tight the fabric might pucker, but the thread will be less visible. The farther you space each stitch apart the more visible the thread will be. Play with the length and tightness of your stitch to find what works best for your project.

## Straight Stitch

Just as easy as it sounds.

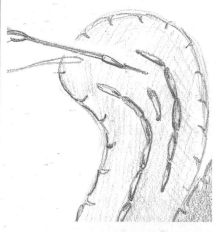

### How to do the straight stitch

Hide your knot between the layers and then bring the needle up and down through both layers of fabric at regular intervals. If you want to make a solid decorative seam, turn back and make a second line of stitches to fill in the spaces in the first seam.

## Satin Stitch

A purely decorative surface stitch that is often used to make leaves and flower petals.

### How to do the satin stitch

Hide your knot under the fabric and begin at the bottom edge, making your first horizontal stitch from left to right. At the right side make a small vertical stitch (⅛" [3mm] or less) under the fabric to lift the needle into position for the horizontal stitch back to the left side. Repeat the small stitch step on the left side; each new horizontal stitch should be positioned above the last. Continue until the satin stitch has filled the desired area and knot the ends under your work.

# needle felt fun

Needle felting is like sculpture for fiber artists. If you've never tried it, you're in for a treat; if you're already an experienced felter, you'll enjoy the new project ideas in this chapter. Needle felting begins with wrapping and forming wool roving into shapes. Place the shaped roving over a brush felting pad and start poking it with a felting needle. The barbs in the needle will intertwine the individual fibers and compress and shape your creation.

The needle-felted forest friends (page 20) and *Mermaids and Fairies* (page 30) in this chapter are all constructed around a twisted chenille stem skeleton. Layers of roving are tightly wrapped around the chenille stems and then repeatedly needle felted. Chenille stems give your finished creation strength and add to the fun since the finished toys can be posed into place.

Needle felt directly into 100% wool felt, which is how the *Gnome Doll* and *Matryoshka Doll* (pages 26 and 29) get their faces. So much quicker than embroidery, you simply roll a small section of roving into eyes and nose shapes and poke them into place. Wool roving can also be needle felted directly into rigid foam—the trick behind making the bumpy pie top on page 36. Whichever technique you choose to start with, enjoy the freedom of creating with loose wool fibers.

Plenty of sewing is also to be had in this chapter. You'll make a tote, little purses that are fun for play, and some delicious-looking strawberries to tempt the eye!

# tree tote with forest friends

This delightful play space makes a gorgeous decoration or can travel with your child on short adventures. Constructed with multiple layers of felt and decorative topstitching, the trunk, branches and leaves hold their shapes without interfacing. Both branch and trunk openings are big enough to accommodate the adventures of the needle-felted squirrel, chipmunk and owl.

Each of the animals has a chenille stem core that allows you to pose their tails and bodies. After you make these critters, you'll discover how easy it is to change the colors and size to add a skunk, or even a raccoon, to your cast of animals.

## Tree Tote Materials

- ➲ Pattern pieces on page 109
- ➲ ¼ yard each of 35% wool felt in brown, beige, light beige for log, branches, stump
- ➲ Two strips 3" × 11" (7.5cm × 28cm) 100% wool felt in sage for handle
- ➲ 8" × 5" (20.5cm × 12.5cm) piece of 100% wool felt in sage for leaves
- ➲ 8" × 5" (20.5cm × 12.5cm) printed cotton for leaves
- ➲ Two acorn caps predrilled with two ⅛" (3mm) holes spaced ¼" (6mm) apart
- ➲ Two 1" (2.5cm) purple felt beads for acorns
- ➲ White thread

## Tools

- ➲ Drill with 1/16" (2mm) bit
- ➲ Hot glue gun and melt sticks
- ➲ Sewing machine
- ➲ Sewing needle
- ➲ Straight pins
- ➲ Scissors
- ➲ Ballpoint pen
- ➲ Marking pen

**Dimensions**
*11" x 10" x 13" (28cm × 25.5cm × 33cm) circumference at the base*

**1** Stack three layers of felt lightest to darkest, and cut the Log, Branches 1 and 2 and the Stump pattern shapes through all three layers of felt. Working on the inside of the log, lightest color facing up, pin the three layers of felt together to stabilize them.

Cut the holes out of the Log pattern and then use a ballpoint pen to trace the circles onto the felt. Pinch the fabric in the center of the hole and snip an opening to insert the scissor points. Cut out all four circles though all three layers of felt (Fig. 1).

**Fig. 1**

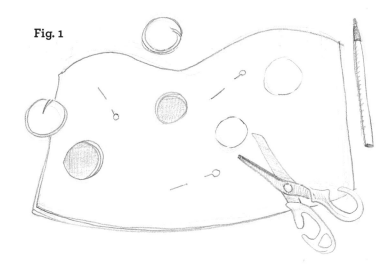

**2** Cut four 1" (2.5cm) wide elongated triangles from the scraps of the brown felt. Pin them around the holes so the widest part rests against the base. Cut additional shorter strips or triangles for the branches.

If you find it helpful, transfer the pattern stitching lines onto the felt with a marking pen. With white thread in the sewing machine, sew vertical stitches up and down the log. Topstitch up and down the piece to create a decorative pattern that also connects the felt layers and seals the openings. (See Freeform Stitching on page 15; to switch the direction of the stitch, see Turning a Corner on page 15.) Repeat this process with each of the branch pieces (Fig. 2).

**Fig. 2**

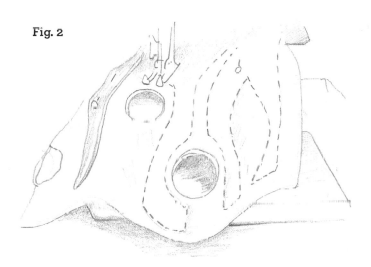

**3** To attach a Branch (either 1 or 2) to the Log, slide the Log, right side up, under the presser foot, positioning the presser foot over the edge of one of the large holes. Slide the base of a Branch against the opening. Stitch around the outside of the opening to connect the Branch to the Log (Fig. 3). Stop when you've encircled the opening. Repeat the process to attach the remaining Branch around the remaining large hole.

**Fig. 3**

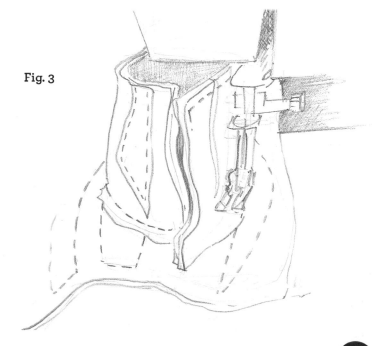

**4** Cut out the Stump from the three layers of felt and pin them together. Transfer the spiral design with a marking pen. Slide the center of the circle under the presser foot. Stitch a spiral, expanding it larger with each rotation; work the fabric around until you reach the outer edge. Turn the Log inside out. With right sides together, curl the bottom edge of the Log around the bottom edge of the Stump base, and sew them together (Fig. 4). Stop stitching after you've encircled the base (Fig. 5). Trim the excess felt from the base, and turn the purse right side out.

**5** Trim and hand stitch the open sides of the branches and log. To do this, work on the right side and position one edge over the other and stitch where the overlap occurs; this will close the openings without adding bulk.

**6** To make the stem handle, fold the sides of the sage felt strip into the middle, overlap one side over the other. It should be $\frac{1}{2}$" (1.5cm) wide. Make a single seam down the center to connect all three layers of felt together. Repeat the process to make a second stem.

**7** Use the Handle Leaf pattern to cut out four leaves, two from printed cotton and two from green felt. Place each felt leaf with a fabric leaf with right sides together, pin and machine stitch around the outside edge of the leaf, leaving a $1\frac{1}{2}$" (4cm) opening at the base of the leaf. Trim off any excess fabric and turn the leaf right side out. As shown on the pattern, topstitch a decorative leaf vein through both layers, beginning your stitching $\frac{1}{2}$" (1.5cm) from the bottom edge of the leaf. Repeat the process to complete the second leaf.

**8** Slip one end of a stem between the fabric and felt at the bottom of the leaf. Tuck under the cut edges of the leaf and hand stitch the opening closed, catching the stem end in your stitches. When finished attaching, pull the needle and thread to the fabric side of the leaf and stitch an acorn cap to the leaf. Knot and trim your thread. Hot glue the felt bead inside the top of the acorn cap.

Repeat the process to connect the second leaf to the second stem.

**9** Find a break in the decorative trunk stitching at the top of the tote and slide the plain end of each stem between the layers of felt. Hand stitch them in place; go over your stitches a couple of times to strengthen the connection. Knot and then trim the excess thread.

Tie the finished handle together in a square knot.

**Fig. 4**

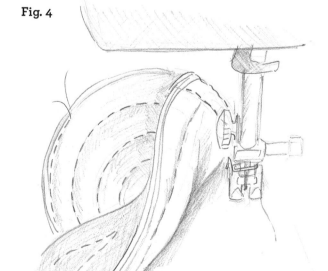

**Fig. 5**

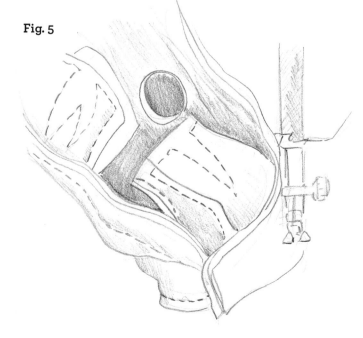

# Owl

You'll be amazed how quick and easy this owl is to needle felt. His little feet are the wrapped chenille stem ends. Winding up his little round body is easy and fun—make him as round as you want.

1  Fold the chenille stem in half and then create a 2" (5cm) high loop by twisting the chenille ends together. The two 1½" (4cm) chenille stem ends become the legs and feet (Fig. 6).

Fold over the very end of the chenille stem and trap the center of a long strand of light brown roving. Tightly wrap one side of the roving around the owl foot, working your way down to the leg. Repeat the wrapping process with the other side of the roving. If necessary add another strand of roving to completely conceal the stem. Use the same technique to wrap and cover the second foot and leg. Needle felt the covered legs over the rigid foam board to hold the roving in place.

2  Fold up the last ½" (1.5cm) of the wrapped chenille to make a double thick ½" (1.5cm) long foot. Bend it at a 90 degree angle to transition up to a ½" (1.5cm) long leg (Fig. 6). Make the same two bends in the second leg.

3  To make the owl's body, encircle the loop with a generous amount of white fill roving. For added stability, alternate wrapping some layers of roving from the top of the head down between the legs and back up again. Continue wrapping until you've created a full round owl shape (Fig. 7). Place the owl on the rigid foam board and needle felt all sides to strengthen the wrapping. Over wrap the owl's head in light brown roving, then needle felt it in place. Place curly white roving over the chest and needle felt it in place.

4  Spiral light brown roving into two 1¾" (4.5cm) long wings and a spiral 2" (5cm) long dark brown tail (Fig. 8). Place each piece on the rigid foam board and

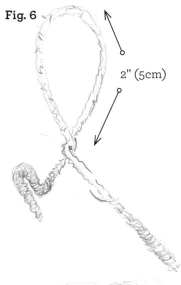

Fig. 6

2" (5cm)

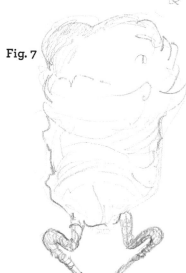

Fig. 7

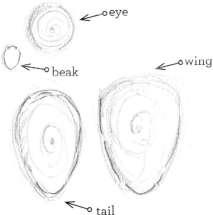

Fig. 8

eye

beak

wing

tail

## Owl Materials

- ⊃ Chenille stem
- ⊃ White fill roving
- ⊃ Roving in buff, light brown, dark brown, black, curly white

## Tools

- ⊃ Felting needle
- ⊃ Needle felting tool
- ⊃ Rigid foam board or brush felting pad

**Dimensions**

4" x 3" (10cm × 7.5cm)

needle felt the spirals on both sides so they hold their shape. Needle felt the top of each wing to either side of the owl, and the top of the tail to the back. All three pieces should connect just below the owl's head and extend down the body.

5  Spiral two ¾" (2cm) outer eyes out of brown roving and needle felt them on the rigid foam board. Spiral two ½" (1.5cm) inner eyes out of buff roving, and two ¼" (6mm) pupils out of black roving. Stack a black pupil over each

buff inner eye and needle felt them to the center of the brown outer eyes. Roll a ¼" (6mm) beak out of dark brown roving and needle felt it on all sides. Next, position the eyes and beak on the owl's face and needle felt them directly into the owl. Make sure you poke all around the base of the beak so it's firmly attached.

# Chipmunk

I love the combination of buff, tan and brown on this little chipmunk—as soon as you add in the black eyes and mouth, his personality takes shape.

**Fig. 8**

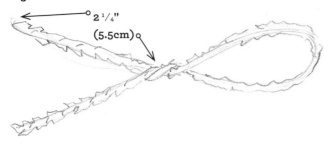

2 ¼" (5.5cm)

**Fig. 9**

**Fig. 10**

**Fig. 11**

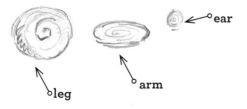

leg

arm

ear

**1** Fold the chenille stem in half and twist the wires together 2 ¼" (5.5cm) from the end (Fig. 8).

**2** Tightly wind strands of white roving around the chenille stem. Build up roundness on the head and body by winding additional layers around those areas (Fig. 9). Completely conceal the chenille stems in the roving. Over wrap the entire body in the light brown color; the body should be 1" (2.5cm) wide at the head and 2" (5cm) wide at the hips.

**3** To make a lifelike tail, needle felt the end of additional vertical strands of roving to the base of the tail. Loosely needle felt the length of the roving pieces so they attach to the first tail layer but still appear bushy and natural (Fig. 10).

**4** Position a long strip of white roving from the nose to the tip of the tail. Lay a thinner strand of dark brown roving down the center of the white strip. Firmly needle felt the decorative stripes in place.

**5** Spiral a ¾" (2cm) long oval of light brown roving to make an arm, lay it on the rigid foam and needle felt it on both sides. Repeat the process and make a second arm. Invert the chipmunk and position half of the arm over the chipmunk's chest. The paw should extend out from the chest. Needle felt the overlapped portion to the chipmunk's belly to secure the arms in place (Fig. 11).

**6** Spiral a generous strand of light brown roving into a 1" (2.5cm) wide thigh for a back haunch. Lay it on the rigid foam board and needle felt it on both sides. Repeat the process to make a second haunch. Tip the chipmunk on its side and needle felt the spiraled haunch to the backside of the body. Flip the chipmunk over and attach the second haunch in the same position on the other side.

**7** Roll tiny amounts of light brown roving into ¼" (6mm) ears, roll an even smaller amount of dark brown roving for a round nose, and two even tinier balls of black roving for the eyes. Needle felt all the balls on the rigid foam board. Position one piece at a time on the chipmunk's face and poke them into position.

## Chipmunk Materials

- ➲ Chenille stem
- ➲ White fill roving
- ➲ Roving on buff, light brown, dark brown, black

## Tools

- ➲ Felting needle
- ➲ Needle felting tool
- ➲ Rigid foam board or brush felting pad

### Dimensions

6" × 2 ¼" (15cm × 5.5cm) at the hips, 1" (2.5cm) at the head, ¾" (2cm) at the neck

# Squirrel

In New England we have gray squirrels. If you live in a part of the world that is populated by red or brown squirrels, please switch colors accordingly.

### Squirrel Instructions

*Follow the chipmunk steps to make the squirrel, incorporating the following adjustments. In step 2, wind additional plain roving to enlarge the width of the hips, head and neck and extend the tail to 3" (7.5cm) long. Slightly increase the size of the ears to ⅓" (1cm), the haunches to 1 ¼" (3cm) and front legs to 1" (2.5cm). Skip the addition of color stripes, and roll black roving into a thin strip to make a W shaped mouth.*

## Squirrel Materials

- ➲ Chenille stem
- ➲ White fill roving
- ➲ Wool roving in white, gray, black

## Tools

- ➲ Felting needle
- ➲ Needle felting tool
- ➲ Rigid foam board or brush felting pad

### Dimensions

7" × 2 ½" (18cm × 6.5cm) wide at the hips, 1 ¼" (3cm) at the head, 1" (2.5cm) wide at the neck

# gnome doll

I've always been captivated by the lore surrounding gnomes. They're known as intelligent beings who care for the animals of the forest. Decked out in his traditional blue coat, brown belt and red hat, this jaunty fellow will happily perch on your shelf or mantle. The 100% wool felt hair and face pieces allow you to needle felt the wool roving facial features and curly beard in place. I've simplified his shape into a weighted cone that can be easily changed into a female version.

## Gnome Materials

- ➲ Pattern pieces on pages 109-110
- ➲ 12" × 9" (30.5cm × 23cm) blue 35% wool felt for body, arms
- ➲ 5" × 5" (12.5cm × 12.5cm) white 100% wool felt for hair
- ➲ 8" × 10" (20.5cm × 25.5cm) red 35% wool felt for hat
- ➲ 5" × 5" (12.5cm × 12.5cm) medium brown 35% wool felt for base, buckle
- ➲ 5" × 5" (12.5cm × 12.5cm) putty 100% wool felt for face, hands
- ➲ ½" × 10" (1.5cm × 25.5cm) strip of dark brown 100% wool felt for belt
- ➲ Wool roving in buff, black, curly white
- ➲ Blue and ochre embroidery floss
- ➲ Blue, white and red sewing thread
- ➲ Fiberfill stuffing
- ➲ Small dried beans

## Tools

- ➲ Sewing machine
- ➲ Crewel and sewing needles
- ➲ Felting needle
- ➲ Straight pins
- ➲ Scissors
- ➲ Rigid foam board or brush felting pad

**Dimensions**

9 ½" × 4 ½" (24cm × 11.5cm), 9" (23cm) *circumference at the base*

**1**  Use the pattern on page 109 to cut the Gnome Body pieces out of blue, the Gnome Front of Hair and Back of Hair pieces out of white, the Gnome Hat pieces out of red, and the Gnome Face out of putty.

Working with the front and back pieces, line the top of each Hair piece with the top edge of each Body piece and pin them in place. Thread the sewing machine with white thread and sew along the bottom edge of each Hair piece. Pin and stitch around the edge of the Face to connect it to the front body piece. Pin the bottom of each Hat piece over the top edge of the hair. Switch to red thread and make a single seam to stitch the Hat pieces in place (Fig. 1).

**2**  Stack the front and back body pieces over each other, right sides together (Fig. 2). Be careful to line up the edges of the hat, hair and body. Sew down both sides using a 1/4" (6mm) seam; leave the curved bottom open.

Trim away any excess fabric, especially off the top of the hat, before turning it right side out. Use a knitting needle or stuffing stick to push the point of the hat right side out.

**3**  Cut the Gnome Base piece out of brown felt. Tightly stuff the top of the hat with fiberfill.

Attach the Base of the gnome before continuing to stuff the rest of the gnome. Pin the bottom edge of the gnome body to the Base piece. Position a section of the pinned felt under the presser foot. Work your way around the base, removing the pins as you reach them. Leave a 2" (5cm) opening, and then end your seam.

Finish stuffing the gnome body with fiberfill. Leave a small space at the base to pour in a quarter cup of dried beans. This will weight the doll and help him stand upright. Hand stitch the opening closed (Fig. 3).

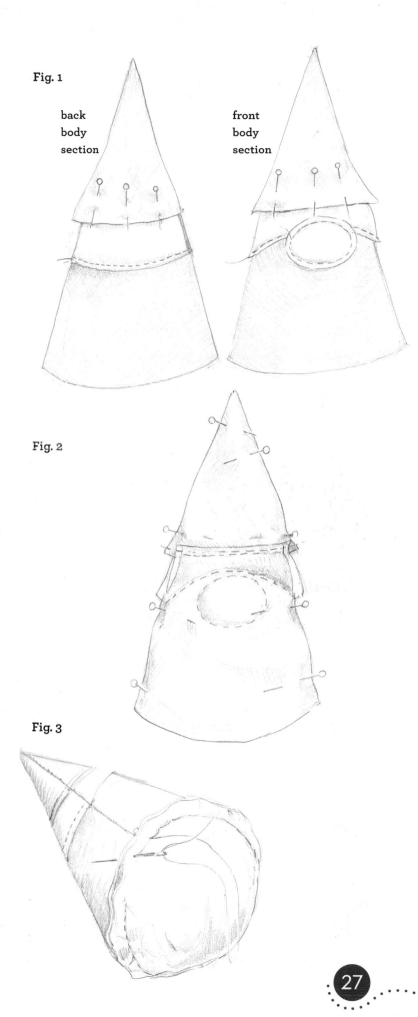

Fig. 1

back body section

front body section

Fig. 2

Fig. 3

**4** Cut the Gnome Belt from dark brown felt and the Gnome Belt Buckle pattern out of medium brown felt. Thread one end of the Belt strip through the slits in the Buckle. Wrap the Belt around the gnome's waist. Use a needle, thread and tiny stitches to tack the overlapped Belt and Buckle in place.

Cut four Gnome Hand patterns out of putty-colored felt, pin each pair right sides together and then seam the outside edges, leaving the straight edge unsewn.

Turn the hand right side out and stuff. Cut two Gnome Arm patterns out of blue felt. Place a hand on the straight edge of the pattern (Fig. 4).

Fold the end of the sleeve around the open edge of the hand and pin to secure (Fig. 5). Hand stitch the folded fabric in place and then hand sew a couple of small stitches to connect the edge of the sleeve to the front of the hand.

Next, stitch the single layer section of the Arm to each side of the gnome. The elbow should overlap the top of the Belt, and the shoulder should rest just below the bottom edge of the Hat.
Repeat the process for the other arm.

**5** Needle felt two tiny rolled pinches of black roving directly into the felt face to make eyes. Needle felt the curly roving directly into the felt face and form a beard at the bottom of the face, and felt curly roving directly onto the hair pieces. Lay the gnome on the rigid foam board and needle felt two ears, two eyebrows and a rolled pea-sized nose out of buff roving. Needle felt the brows to the top of the face piece, the nose above the beard, and tuck the ears behind the edge of the face (Fig. 6).

**6** Use a full strand of blue floss to blanket stitch around the bottom edge of the doll. Use a full strand of ochre floss to make a single straight stitch to complete the belt detail.

Fig. 4

Fig. 5

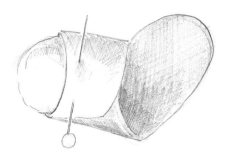

Fig. 6

# Matryoshka Doll

Whether you make a partner for your gnome or decide to make a set of stand-alone Nordic-inspired matryoshka dolls, the assembly is almost the same as the gnome. You can easily modify the height of the doll pattern to make a set of dolls that range from smallest to tallest.

## Matryoshka Materials

- Pattern pieces on page 109-110
- 4 ½" × 9" (11.5cm × 23cm) blue 35% wool felt for cape
- 6" × 5" (15cm × 12.5cm) printed cotton for shirt
- 5 ½" × 5" (14cm × 12.5cm) orange 100% wool felt for skirt
- 3 ½" × 3 ½" (9cm × 9cm) green 35% wool felt for collar placard
- 2 ½" × 2 ½" (6.5cm × 6.5cm) putty 100% wool felt for face
- 3" × 3" (7.5cm × 7.5cm) dark brown 100% wool felt for hair
- 8" × 5" (20.5cm × 12.5cm) red 35% wool felt for sleeves, base
- Wool roving in butt, dark brown, red
- Tiny felt flowers
- E glass beads
- Red embroidery thread
- Red, blue and white thread

## Tools

- Pinking shears
- Sewing machine
- Crewel and sewing needles
- Felting needle
- Straight pins
- Scissors
- Rigid foam board or brush felting pad

## Matryoshka Instructions

*Substitute the Hood for the gnome's hat, and the fabric Shirt and felt Skirt for his body.*

Overlap the bottom of the felt Hood and the top of the felt Skirt over the fabric Shirt. Pin and stitch the pieces together. Cut the Collar Placard template out with pinking shears and position it at the base of the Cape on the front body piece so it extends over the center front of the shirt. Machine stitch the placard section that extends over the shirt in place. Center the Face (cut from putty felt) in the round portion of the Collar Placard, pin and stitch it in place. Cut out the Hair pattern from the dark brown felt, and pin and stitch it to the top of the Face. Allow the ends of the pigtails to hang free.

Follow steps 2-4 to join the body pieces, add stuffing, add the Base and Arms. Skip the instructions for the Belt. Needle felt the dark brown roving to the Hair piece. Place it on the rigid foam board to add roving to the ends of the pigtails. Roll two tiny black eyes and a small red mouth, and then needle felt them to the face; use the putty roving to make round cheeks. Use a sewing needle and thread to hand stitch a tiny flower and E bead center to the top of the cape and another set to the placard section of the collar. Just as you did for the gnome, blanket stitch around the bottom edge of the dress.

# mermaids and fairies

Fairies and mermaids make wonderful additions to playtime. Needle felting makes it easy to achieve soft and pliable characters for the imaginative child in your life. As a bonus, they can go wherever she does with the addition of a carry-along purse.

Both the fairy and the mermaid start and finish the same way. I split up step 5 to reflect the difference of making legs versus making a tail.

## Materials

### Fairy

- ⤷ Pattern pieces for wings on pages 110
- ⤷ 1 1/2 chenille stems in beige
- ⤷ Wavy pink roving for hair
- ⤷ White fill roving
- ⤷ Wool roving in flesh tones, dark brown, blue, red, pink
- ⤷ Felt scraps in mauve, light and dark pink for flowers

### Mermaid

- ⤷ Use all the same materials and tools listed above but switch the fabric and roving colors to:
- ⤷ Wavy blue roving for hair
- ⤷ Wool roving in flesh tones, dark brown, light blue, dark and light aqua, green
- ⤷ Felt scraps in turquoise, light blue, light aqua for flowers

## Tools

- ⤷ Pen-style felting tool
- ⤷ Felting needle
- ⤷ Rigid foam board or brush felting pad
- ⤷ Die cut machine with flower dies in various sizes, at least 1 1/2" (4cm) in diameter
- ⤷ Scissors
- ⤷ Sewing machine
- ⤷ Hot glue gun and melt sticks

## Dimensions

*Fairy: 5 1/4" (13.5cm) tall*
*Mermaid: 6 1/2" (16.5cm) tall*

## TIP

Save your scissors: use wire cutters to cut the chenille stems.

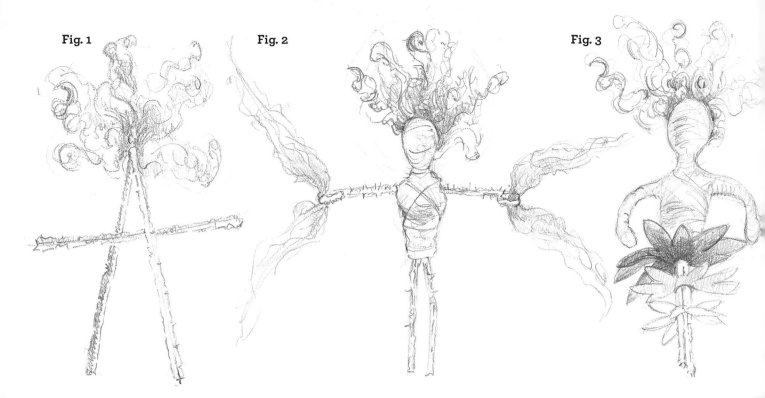

Fig. 1  Fig. 2  Fig. 3

**1** Fold the long chenille stem in half. Trap the center of a generous pinch of the curly hair roving in the fold. Tightly twist the chenille stem to secure the hair. Insert the half stem for the arms between the two chenille stem ends approximately 1 ¼" (3cm) from the hair twist (Fig. 1).

**2** Tightly wrap white fill roving under the hair to create a head shape. Continue winding small pinches of roving around the center of the head until you're pleased with the shape. Wrap a small amount of roving around the neck and then switch to a diagonal wrapping technique to fill the chest area and stabilize the arms. Wrap from the right shoulder down to the left armpit and then reverse, wrapping from the left shoulder to the right armpit. Working on the rigid foam board, needle felt all sides of the head, neck and chest to compress the fibers (Fig. 2).

**3** Fold over the last ½" (1.5cm) of the arms to make the hands. Trap the center of a long strand of flesh tone roving inside each hand (Fig. 2). Wrap one end at a time around the folded chenille stem. Continue wrapping down the length of the arm. Repeat the process with the other side of the roving strand, overlapping your first wraps. Wrap the other hand in a similar fashion.

**4** Pull out more strands of flesh tone roving and wrap them over the white face and neck. Continue adding and needle felting layers until the white roving is completely covered. Next, encircle the torso with the flesh tone roving, working from top to bottom. It's important to wrap the ends around the shoulders and down the arms—this will add thickness to the top of the arms and integrate them with the body. Finally, add more strands down the length of the arms to fill them out.

Using the die cut machine, cut out three felt flowers from the assorted felt scraps. Cut a small hole in the center of each flower. Bring the chenille stems together and thread them through three felt flowers. (Fig. 3).

**5** *To make the fairy legs: (Fig. 4)*
Separate the chenille stem ends to form two legs. Like the arms, fold up ½" (1.5cm) of each leg to make a foot. Trap a strand of flesh tone roving in each fold. Tightly wrap one end of the strand around the folded chenille stem foot. Continue wrapping the roving up toward the leg. Wrap the other side of the roving around the foot and leg, and needle felt the wraps to hold them in place.

Repeat the process with the other leg, and then add additional strands of flesh tone roving to fill out both legs. Switch to blue roving and over wrap the flesh tone legs to dress your fairy in blue leggings. Be sure to make several wraps around the top of

**Fig. 4**

**TIP**

It's easy to make the eyes too big. To fix, simply use your needle end to pull the eyes out. Start again with a smaller ball of roving.

**Fig. 5**

the legs just under the flower skirt to give your fairy hips. Needle felt the legs from top to bottom to tightly join the blue leggings.

*To make the mermaid tail: (Fig. 5)*

Twist the chenille stems together 1" (2.5cm) from the ends. Begin forming the tail shape with white fill roving. Tightly wrap roving strands just below the flowers, working your way down toward the twist at the end of the tail. Continue adding more strands of fill roving around the hips, wrapping the thinner ends toward the bottom of the tail. Place the mermaid on the rigid foam board and needle felt the fill roving on all sides to give the tail a solid base.

To form the flippers turn up the bottom ¼" (6mm) of the chenille stem ends and trap the center of a dark aqua roving strand in each fold. Tightly wrap each end of the strand around the folded chenille ends to fill out the flippers. Wrap additional strands of aqua around the flippers, then continue

wrapping the roving ends up around the twisted chenille. Over wrap the remaining white fill with a combination of light and dark aqua roving. Needle felt each flipper and the length of the tail on all sides.

**6** Finish dressing your fairy or mermaid by wrapping the torso with a generous strand of colored roving. The roving bodice should cover the chest and stretch all the way down to the flower skirts. Needle felt the bodice on all sides to firmly attach it to the flesh tone roving. Spiral tiny strands of roving into small flowers and needle felt them to the top of the bodice. Embellish the flowers with even smaller rolled strands of lighter colored roving to make the flower centers. To add even more detail, needle felt tiny leaves around the flowers.

**7** Roll small, round eyes from tiny strands of dark brown roving. Needle felt them directly into

the eyes. Roll a strand of red or pink roving into a ⅓" (1cm) long oval for the lips. Needle felt it to the face. Use the needle tip to pull flesh tone roving down over the center of the red/pink lips to help shape them. You can use the same trick on either side pulling flesh tone roving up at the corners of the mouth to upturn the edges into a smile. Once you're happy with the face you can flatten the hair over the back of the head. Carefully needle felt it in place. Be sure you don't poke it all the way through the head, or you will poke out the face. Frame the hair around the face by poking it down on the sides.

**8** For the fairy, cut a pair of Wings out of light and dark pink felt. Pin them together and topstitch around the edges. Lift up the fairy's hair and hot glue the wings to the fairy back (alternatively you could hand stitch them in place).

# Flower Purse

Fairies are keepers of flowers. Stitch up a pretty blossom for them to sleep and play in. This quick little project will add charm and value to your needle-felted creation.

**Fig. 6**

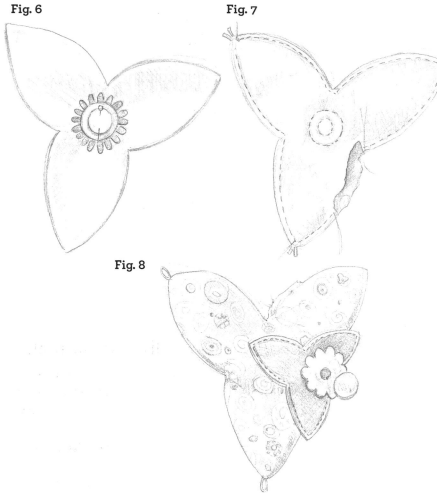

**Fig. 7**

**Fig. 8**

## Flower Purse Materials

- ➲ Pattern pieces on page 111
- ➲ Pink felt
- ➲ Printed pink cotton
- ➲ Felt scraps in light and dark blue, yellow, dark pink, green, at least 3" (7.5cm) square for flower and circle embellishments
- ➲ White elastic cord
- ➲ Large round pink bead
- ➲ Yellow plastic flower

## Tools

- ➲ Sewing needle and thread
- ➲ Sewing machine
- ➲ Die cut machine with 1" (2.5cm) and 1½" (4.5cm) circle dies and 2½" (6cm) flower dies
- ➲ Scissors
- ➲ Straight pins

**Dimensions**
5" × 5" (12.5cm × 12.5cm)

**1** Use the patterns as your guide to cut Flower Purse Layer 1 out of pink felt and patterned pink fabric. Die cut one 2½" (6cm) flower and one of each size circles from the scrap felts. Stack the flower, large circle and small circle and pin them to the center of the pink felt flower. Machine stitch around the inside edge of the circle to anchor the embellishments in place (Fig. 6).

**2** Placing right sides together, stack the cotton petal over the felt petal. Insert a folded 1¼" (3cm) section of elastic cord into two of the petal points. Pin them in place so that ¼" (6mm) of the cord ends emerge out the top. The bend will be trapped in the insides. Machine stitch around the edge of the petals, trapping the cord ends in the seam. Leave a 3" (7.5cm) opening to turn the piece. Turn it right side out (Fig. 7). Hand stitch the opening closed, tucking in the cut edges so you match the machine seam. Return to the sewing machine and topstitch around the edge of the petals.

**3** Cut Flower Purse Inner Petals out of light and dark pink felt, pin the two layers together and topstitch them together around the inside edge. Die cut one 2½" (6cm) flower and a 1" (2.5cm) circle from the scrap felts. Stack the felt circle on top of the felt flower and pin them to the center of the dark pink side. Machine stitch around the inside edge of the circle to anchor the embellishments in place, and set the small petals aside. Lay the small dark pink petals over the center of the patterned fabric petals. Offset the small petals so they fall between the large ones (Fig. 8). Hand stitch the center of small dark pink petals to the patterned fabric. Stitch a plastic flower and large round bead to the petal point without a loop. Hook the loops over the bead to open and close the flower.

# Shell Purse

Don't leave your mermaid out in the cold. A simple bivalve shell purse unhinges to let her hide inside. A pearl and flower bead combination forms a decorative loop closure.

**Fig. 9**

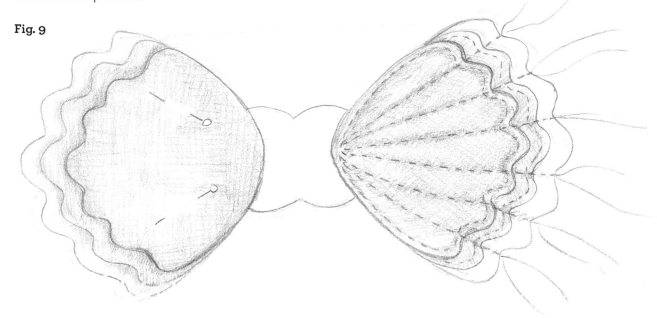

**1** Fold your white felt in half and align the edge of the Shell Purse Layer 1 pattern along the fold in the felt and cut out the shell pattern through both layers. Repeat the process to cut a second double white shell. Fold the light blue and light aqua felt to cut out two pieces each of Shell Purse Layer 2 (light blue) and Shell Purse Layer 3 (light aqua).

**2** Outstretch one of the connected white shells and stack the light blue and aqua shells over the large white shells. Pin the layers in place, and follow the lines indicated on the pattern to machine stitch the layers together. First, stitch along the scalloped edge of the light blue and aqua shells, then make diagonal seams through all three layers to delineate the valleys along the top of each scallop layer (Fig. 9).

**3** Position the second white shell under the first and pin through all the layers. Cut a 1 1/4" (3cm) piece of elastic cord, fold it in half, and push the ends between the layers on one side of the shell. Pin the cord in place. Topstitch the top edges of the white shell together. If necessary, move the sides of the blue and aqua shell layers out of the way so they don't get caught in the seam. Make sure the elastic cording is trapped in the seam.

**4** Using a sewing needle threaded with white thread, hand stitch the hinge of the shell together. Continue stitching up the sides of the shell to connect the front and back of the purse together. Reinforce the connection by turning the purse inside out and making a second seam on the inside. Hand stitch the flower and bead closure to the top front of the purse. Lift the elastic loop over the bead and flower to open and close the purse.

## Shell Purse Materials

- Pattern pieces on page 110
- 12" × 6" (30.5cm × 15cm) pieces of 35% wool felt in white, light blue, light aqua
- Blue and white plastic flower beads
- White elastic cord

## Tools

- Sewing thread and needle
- Sewing machine
- Scissors
- Straight pins

### Dimensions
5 3/4" × 5 3/4" (14.5cm × 14.5cm)

# cherry strawberry pie

This is low-calorie baking at its finest. Fabric and felt combine to make a scrumptious, decorative, deep-dish pie. Instead of being left with a plate of crumbs you'll enjoy your handiwork for years to come. Sections of rigid foam disk make the firm triangular wedges, and small Styrofoam balls create the bumpy top. Once you see how quickly they stitch together you'll be inspired to stitch a play version with different colored fruit fabric slices.

## Pie Piece Materials

- ➲ Pattern pieces on pages 111-112
- ➲ 8" (20.5cm) diameter, 2" (5cm) thick Styrofoam disk
- ➲ Assorted red printed fabrics (I used six different prints in the same color families)
- ➲ 100% wool felt in caramel, putty
- ➲ 1" (2.5cm) Styrofoam balls (three to four per pie crust, 18-24 total)
- ➲ White fill wool roving
- ➲ Embroidery floss in tan
- ➲ Sewing thread

## Tools

- ➲ Sewing machine
- ➲ Sewing needle
- ➲ Straight pins
- ➲ Scissors
- ➲ Kitchen knife
- ➲ Felting needle or three-needle tool
- ➲ Measuring tape
- ➲ Rigid foam board or brush felting pad
- ➲ Pencil

### Dimensions

*Makes a five-slice, 9 1/4" (23.5cm) diameter pie with a sixth piece for sharing*
*Each pie slice: 5" x 4 1/2" x 3 1/4" (12.5cm × 11.5cm × 8.5cm)*

**1** Working over a protected surface, use the kitchen knife to cut the Styrofoam disc in half. Wrap the measuring tape around the outside of the Styrofoam disc and use a pencil to mark every 4" (10cm). Move the tape to the inside and lay it across the flat edge. Mark the center of the pie. Line up the length of the knife blade with the outside markings and the center mark to cut each half into three wedges (Fig. 1).

**2** Use the pattern to cut the Pie Filling and a Pie Top piece out of printed cotton. Use the Pie Top and Bottom pattern to cut a caramel felt Pie Bottom; cut the Back of Crust piece from caramel felt.
   Fold the filling fabric widthwise right sides together, pin it and stitch a straight seam along the fold.

**3** Placing right sides together align the bottom edge of one side of the Pie Filling with the edge of the felt Pie Bottom piece. Pin and stitch the edges together (Fig. 2). Repeat the process to attach the other side of the Pie Filling to the other side of the felt Pie Bottom.

**4** Keeping right sides together, align the back edge of the felt Pie Bottom over the felt Back of Crust piece. Pin and stitch the two felt pieces together. Next, pin the edge of the Pie Filling to the sides of the Back of Crust and make a separate seam to attach them.

**5** With right side together, pin the fabric Pie Top to the sides of the top edge of the Pie Filling and then stitch. Leave the back edge unsewn to turn it right side out (Fig. 3). Check your seams and trim the corners and edges. Turn the piece right side out.

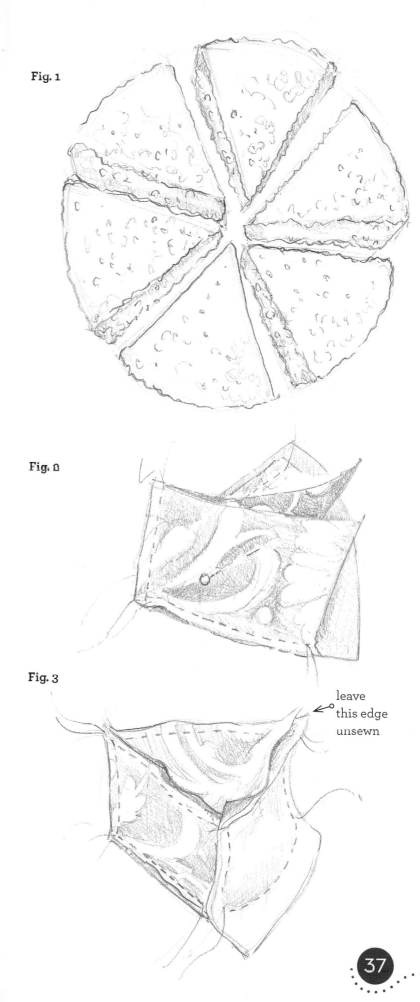

Fig. 1

Fig. 2

Fig. 3

leave this edge unsewn

**6** Insert a Styrofoam wedge, small end first, in the opening between the Back of Crust and Pie Top. Slowly ease it into place, compressing the Styrofoam at the edges (Fig. 4).

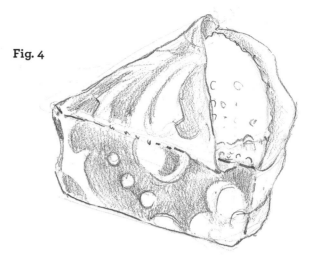

**Fig. 4**

**7** To make the top of the pie crust, use the Pie Crust Top pattern to cut a light colored inside top piece and a caramel colored top. Align and pin the point in the two pieces, and then pin the sides together. Machine stitch the sides, leaving the back edge open. Check your seam and trim the point. Turn the piece right side out.

**8** Position two thin layers of wool roving between the felt. Insert three to four 1" (2.5cm) Styrofoam balls in between the layers of the pie crust top and the wool roving (Fig. 5). Working over the rigid foam board, use the needle felting tool to compress the layers of felt, Styrofoam and roving together. Keep poking until the felt contours the round shape of the balls.

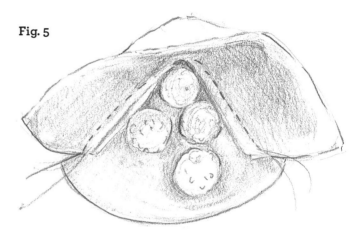

**Fig. 5**

**9** Lay the crust top over the fabric top of the pie, lining up the points of the pie and crust. Fold the open end of the Pie Crust Top down over the back edge of the pie, sandwiching the fabric and felt edges in the fold and creating an edge to the crust. Pin it in place. Thread a crewel needle with a full strand of embroidery floss and stitch along the pinned line, trapping all the layers in the seam (Fig. 6). Switch to a regular needle and red sewing thread to hand stitch the top of the filling to the underside of the crust. Repeat the process from the five remaining slices.

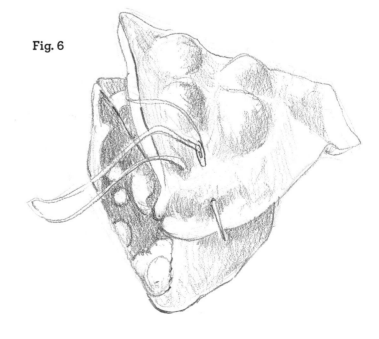

**Fig. 6**

# Strawberries

These sweet little fabric and felt strawberries are so fun; consider stitching up a batch to place in a small wooden carton. Individual strawberries could be placed in different arrangements and paired with different patterned pie slices. If you're stitching them for children skip the bead seeds that might pose a choking hazard.

## Strawberries Materials

- ➲ Pattern pieces and diagram on page 111
- ➲ Scraps of the six red fabrics
- ➲ Fiberfill
- ➲ 35% wool felt in green
- ➲ 7mm green pom-poms
- ➲ Red E seed beads

## Tools

- ➲ Scissors
- ➲ Sewing needle
- ➲ Thread

### Dimensions

1³/₄" × 1¹/₂" (4.5cm × 4cm)

### Strawberry Instructions

*Use the Strawberry pattern to cut three pieces of printed cotton fabric for each strawberry. Pin them right sides together, and stitch all three sides together leaving an opening at the top. Check the seams and trim away the excess fabric. Turn the piece right side out and stuff with fiberfill.*

*Cut the Strawberry Top from the green felt.*

*Hand stitch the top of the strawberry closed and then draw the needle up the center top of the strawberry. String the center of the strawberry leaf and a green pom-pom onto the needle. Slide them down so they rest on the top of the strawberry, then poke the needle back down through the layers. Pull the needle back out through one of the strawberry sides. Thread a red E bead onto the needle and insert the needle*

*back into the strawberry. Continue working this way until you've stitched a few seed beads onto each side of the strawberry. Knot the thread ends under the strawberry leaf and trim away the thread.*

# zipper flowers

These surprising little flowers are quick and easy to stitch together. Folded felt petals give the flowers a uniform look without using a die cut machine. Recycled sweater felt or rolled felt beads give substance to the flower centers while zipper teeth add the sparkle. This versatile little flower can stand alone as a pin, adorn a headband or embellish a bag.

## Flower Pin

Dress up a coat or tote with this snazzy brooch.

## Materials

- ⟳ 1 1/2 " × 16" (4cm × 40.5cm) strip of red felt
- ⟳ 3/4" (2cm) circle of red wool scrap (I suggest a felted wool sweater)
- ⟳ 1 1/8" (3cm) circle of pink felt
- ⟳ Scrap of 35% wool felt in green
- ⟳ Metal zipper (can be salvaged from clothing or purchased at a fabric store; cut off the length you need from one side of the zipper)
- ⟳ 1" (2.5cm) metal pin back

## Tools

- ⟳ Sewing machine
- ⟳ Sewing needle
- ⟳ Straight pins
- ⟳ Scissors

### Dimensions
2" (5cm) round flower with 1 1/2" (4cm) leaf

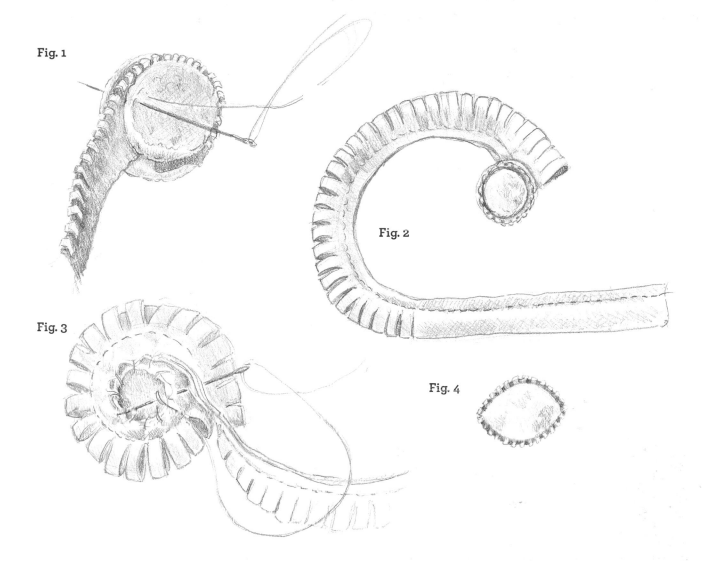

**Fig. 1**

**Fig. 2**

**Fig. 3**

**Fig. 4**

**1** Fold the red strip of felt in half lengthwise, pin the layers together and machine stitch down one edge. Your strip will have a double thickness and will be ³/₄" (2cm) wide. Cut slits ¹/₄" (6mm) apart along the folded edge, being careful not to cut through the stitched seam; the loops will become the petals of your finished flower.

**2** Sandwich a zipper section between the red recycled wool circle and the pink felt circle. Hand stitch along the outer edge of the felt circle, trapping the woven zipper binding between the felt layers (Fig. 1). The metal zipper teeth should rest along the edge of the red wool, and the

pink felt should peek out from behind the zipper teeth. After completing the circle, trim off any additional zipper length, making sure the first and last zipper teeth line up.

**3** Turn the finished flower center over and begin hand stitching the seam side of the petals to the underside of the flower center (Fig. 2). Continue working your way around the flower until you have made three rotations and three layers of petals (Fig. 3). If necessary, cut away the remaining petal strip.

**4** To make the leaf, cut two 1³/₄" × 1¹/₄" (4.5cm × 3cm) green felt

leaf shapes. Sandwich the zipper between one side of the two leaf layers. Beginning at one point of the leaf, hand stitch from the one leaf edge across to the other, trapping the zipper in your stitches. When you reach the other leaf point, fold the zipper down and continue stitching it in place between the edges of the leaves. Trim the zipper when you can determine the necessary length needed to line up with the first zipper tooth (Fig. 4). Hand stitch one point of the leaf to the back of the flower, then secure the pin back with more stitches.

# Snap Pouch

This simple little pouch uses a versatile spring clasp closure. With no zippers or snaps it is a cinch to sew. All that is required is a fabric channel. This little bag is long enough to fit a pair of glasses or an assortment of cosmetics. You can easily adapt the length and size of the fabric to accommodate any size spring clasp.

## Materials

- 9 ½" × 8" (24cm × 20.5cm) white cotton fabric with black spots for lining
- 9 ½" × 8" (24cm × 20.5cm) black, pink and aqua striped cotton fabric for outside
- 3 ¾" (9.5cm) long spring clasp
- Zipper flower made from 2" × 14" (5cm × 35.5cm) strip of 35% pink felt with a blue felt bead (cut in half with scissors) for the center of the flower; Green felt scraps for the leaf (see instructions on page 41; omit the pin back)

## Tools

- Sewing needle and thread
- Sewing machine
- Straight pins
- Scissors

**Dimensions**

6" × 4 ¼" (15cm × 11cm)

Fig. 5

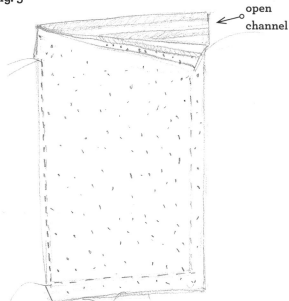

open channel

Fig.6

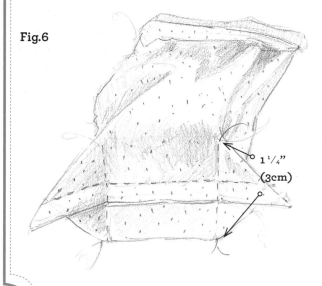

1 ¼" (3cm)

**1** To connect the lining fabric to the outside fabric, place right sides together and pin. Machine stitch one short edge together, turn the piece right side out and iron the seam flat.

The striped fabric is the outside of the pouch and the dotted fabric is the lining. Fold the fabric in half widthwise with the lining side out. The stitched seam should remain at the top. Pin all four layers of fabric together. Beginning 1" (2.5cm) from the top edge, machine stitch the open sides together. When you reach the corner, set the needle (see Turning a Corner on page 15 for instructions). Stitch along the bottom and up the folded edge. End the seam 1" (2.5cm) from the top, leaving an open channel for the spring clasp (Fig. 5).

**2** Pull out the corners to flatten the bottom of the pouch. Make two separate straight seams that intersect the bottom seam 1 ¼" (3cm) from the corners. These seams will give the pouch a square base (Fig. 6). Turn the pouch right side out.

**3** Thread one end of the unfastened snap closure through the opening in the channel at the top inch of the pouch. Keep pushing it through until it emerges out the opening on the other

**Fig. 7**

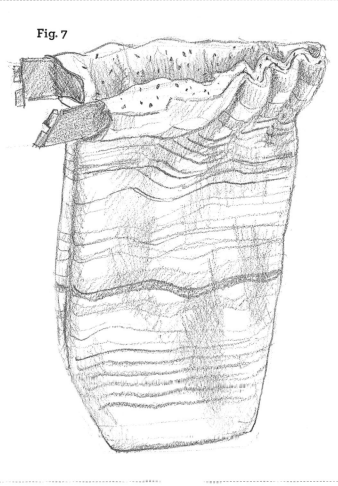

side (Fig. 7). Bring the two ends together and thread the pin through the metal loops. Hand stitch the opening closed, continuing the appearance of the machine stitched seam.

**4** The zipper flower embellishment is made like the pin. Switch the petals to a 2" (5cm) strip of pink felt folded and stitched to a 1" (2.5cm) width. The smaller petal width requires you to place the cuts ¹⁄₈" (3mm) apart. Switch the half felt bead for the recycled wool circle and skip the second felt circle backing. Sandwich the zipper between the head and the petals. Shrink the leaf to 1 ¼" (3cm) long by 1" (2.5cm) wide. Stitch the finished leaf and flower to the center top of the pouch.

# Headband

Small zipper flowers brighten up any hairdo. You can just as easily stitch them to barrettes or hair clips. Felt makes a lovely warm winter hair accessory. For summertime, skip the zipper and switch the felt for fabric. If you back the fabric with interfacing, you'll add weight and prevent fraying.

### Headband Instructions

*Make the flower as you did the pin, shrinking the petal strip to a 1 ½" (4cm) strip; the petals are still cut apart at ¹⁄₈" (3mm) intervals. The leaf shrinks further to be 1" × ¾" (2.5cm × 2cm). Stitch the underside of the finished flower and leaf to one side of the woven headband.*

## Materials

- ⟳ Zipper flower using 1 ½" × 14" (4cm × 35.5cm) 35% wool blue felt strip, half a red felt bead for the center and 35% wool felt green scrap for the leaf (see instructions on page 41; omit the pin back)
- ⟳ Woven headband

## Tools

- ⟳ Sewing needle and thread
- ⟳ Sewing machine
- ⟳ Straight pin

## Chapter Two

# whimsy for the home

**S**ewing has come a long way. No longer limited to needles, scissors and fabric, you can break out your crafting materials and transform your fabric stash into whimsical home accents. Unconventional stuffing materials like wood, Styrofoam, cardboard and chenille stems give lightweight fabrics structure. The soft fabric *Tabletop Trees* (page 54) are supported by dowel rod trunks and stabilized by a solid wood base. Cut and folded posterboard forms the internal structure for *Fanciful Houses* (page 62), and chenille stems help support felt deer legs and antlers (page 58).

One layer of felt is pretty, but multiple layers of complementary colors are stunning, especially when they're sewn onto beautiful fabric. Because cut felt doesn't fray, it lends itself to appliqué projects like the *Mushroom Canvas* (page 50), with no worry about finishing the edges. Felt also has the weight, strength and integrity to stand alone. A series of felt circles quickly becomes a decorative deer garland when overlapped and stitched through the sewing machine. The *Woodland Animal Ornaments* (page 46) are simply made by stacking layers of cut felt pieces.

Want to add even more color for your fabric and felt creations? Decorative embroidery stitches are a great way to give a project a finished look while adding to the handmade appeal.

Stretch the boundaries of conventional sewing and create whimsical, three-dimensional fun for your home.

# woodland animal ornaments

During our first Christmas in Maine, we purchased a beautiful collection of glass animals that are the inspirations for this collection. Deceptively easy to make, these creatures are simply cut from the pattern pieces, layered and hand stitched together at the edges. A few decorative embroidery stitches, wooden bead noses and glass bead eyes make the perfect finishing touches. These beauties don't need to go into hiding after the holidays—they're ideal for felt board play!

## Squirrel Materials

- Pattern pieces on pages 112-113 (do not need seam allowance)
- Embroidery floss in caramel, medium brown, beige
- ¼ yard 35% wool felt in dark brown, medium brown, light ochre
- 6mm round wood beads
- Black glass seed and slightly larger E beads

## Tools

- Sewing and crewel needles
- Straight pins
- Scissors

### Dimensions

5" × 4 ½" (12.5cm × 11.5cm)

# Squirrel

This bushy-tailed squirrel is up on his haunches sniffing the air, ready to hop off and dig up his stash of nuts.

**1** Carefully cut each squirrel pattern piece out of the dark, medium and light felt colors as indicated on the patterns, do not add a seam allowance (Fig. 1). Stack the pieces on top of each other in the numbered order, number one being the base piece. Pin the layers of stacked felt in place to prevent pieces from shifting while you sew.

**2** Use a single strand of caramel colored floss to whipstitch around the outside edge of the tail (see Whipstitch on page 17). Work your way around the base of the tail and then continue stitching around the front foot. Pass the needle behind the stomach and stitch the first two layers together. Connect the second foot, backside of the body and one of the front legs together. End at the squirrel's neck (Fig. 2).

**3** Switch to a single strand of beige floss to stitch up the top two layers of the stomach. Stop at the nose and stitch the wooden bead in place. Change to a small tacking stitch to hold the inside edge of the beige stomach in place.

**Fig. 1**

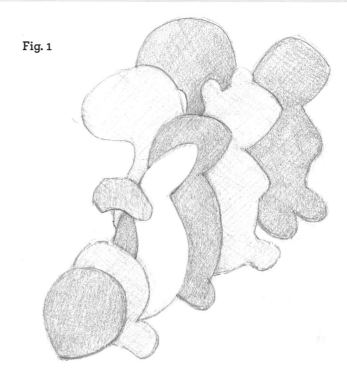

**Fig. 2**

**4** Use a single strand of brown floss to stitch on the eyes, placing a larger eye in the front and a smaller eye toward the back. Make multiple stitches to make a ¼" (6mm) mouth. Use the remaining thread to stitch around the squirrel's back and around the edges of the front paws.

**5** Use a double strand of beige floss to add three lines of decorative stitches up the length of the tail (Fig. 3). Stitch a hanging thread to the top of your finished animal, cut the ends to the desired length and then tie in an overhand knot.

**Fig. 3**

# Rabbit

This sweet snowshoe hare blends in with a winter wonderland.

### Rabbit Instructions

*Cut out the pieces as marked in the light, medium and dark felts. Stack the pieces together as numbered, and pin them together. Use a single thickness of off-white thread to whipstitch around the entire outside of the rabbit. Use smaller tacking stitches to attach the inside of the legs and stomach pieces, stopping to add a single E bead for the eye and a light colored wooden bead for the nose. Use beige thread to make a ¼" (6mm) mouth. Switch to two strands of off-white thread to make three ½" (1.5cm) long whiskers across the cheek and five ½" (1.5cm) long decorative stitches on the tail.*

## Rabbit Materials

- ➲ Pattern pieces on page 113
- ➲ 100% wool felt in buff and white
- ➲ 35% wool felt in light beige
- ➲ Embroidery floss in light brown, off-white
- ➲ Black E bead
- ➲ Small light wood bead

## Tools (for all remaining creatures)

- ➲ Sewing needle
- ➲ Crewel needle
- ➲ Straight pins
- ➲ Scissors

**Dimensions**
5" × 4½" (12.5cm × 11.5cm)

# Deer

Who can resist sighting a sweet doe?

### Deer Instructions

*Cut out the pieces as marked in the light, medium and dark colors. Fold the fabric in half to snip small openings in the back piece. Stack the pieces together as numbered, and then pin them together. Use a single thickness of brown thread to whipstitch around the entire outside of the deer. Use smaller tacking stitches to attach the eye and back piece, stopping to add a single E bead for the eye and a dark colored wooden bead for the nose. Use dark brown thread to make a $\frac{1}{4}$" (6mm) mouth. Switch to two strands of off-white thread to make three $\frac{1}{4}$" (6mm) long decorative stitches up the tail.*

# Fox

This jaunty fellow is ready to dash back into hiding.

### Fox Instructions

*Cut out the pieces as marked in the patterns from the putty and burgundy felt. Stack the pieces together as numbered, and then pin them together. Use a single thickness of maroon thread to whipstitch around the entire outside of the fox. Like the squirrel, the two layers of the front and back legs are stitched together separately. Use smaller tacking stitches to attach the maroon colored headpiece. Stitch a small bead eye in the back, a larger bead eye in the front, and a dark colored wooden bead for the nose. Use dark brown thread to make a $\frac{1}{4}$" (6mm) mouth. Switch to two strands of off-white thread to make a series of straight whiskers that span between the putty and maroon felt on the face and a second set of tail stitches that span between the first two layers. Switch to maroon thread to make a second series of decorative whisker and tail stitches.*

# Hedgehog

We live with porcupines, but European hedgehogs are much more endearing!

### Hedgehog Instructions

*Cut out the pieces as marked in the light, medium and dark colors. Fold the fabric in half to snip small openings in the back piece. Stack the pieces together as numbered. Be sure the beige ear pokes out over the brown back layers, and then pin them together. Use a single thickness of beige thread to whipstitch around the head and feet. Switch to a single strand of medium or dark brown thread to stitch around the back. Use small tacking stitches around the two top brown layers. Continue using medium or dark brown thread to sew a large eye bead to the front of the face, a small eye to the back, and a dark wooden bead nose. End by making a $\frac{1}{2}$" (1.5cm) dark brown mouth.*

## Deer Materials

- Pattern pieces on page 114
- 35% wool felt in brown
- 100% wool felt in caramel, white
- Embroidery floss in off-white, brown
- Black E bead
- Small dark wood bead

**Dimensions**

$5\frac{1}{4}$" × $6\frac{1}{4}$" (13.5cm × 16cm)

## Fox Materials

- Pattern pieces on page 115
- 100% wool felt in putty
- 35% burgundy felt
- Embroidery floss in maroon, off-white, dark brown
- Black glass seed and slightly larger E beads
- Small dark wood bead

**Dimensions**

7" × 5" (18cm × 12.5cm)

## Hedgehog Materials

- Pattern pieces on page 115
- 35% wool felt in beige, medium brown
- 100% wool in dark brown
- Embroidery floss in beige, medium brown, dark brown
- Black glass seed and slightly larger E beads
- Small dark wood bead

**Dimensions**

5" × $3\frac{1}{2}$" (12.5cm × 9cm)

# mushroom canvas

Stitch up whimsical art for your walls. Iron-on fleece and simple machine stitching adds dimension to plain cotton fabric. Felt is the ideal material for appliqué, especially cute mushroom tops from an assortment of colored scraps. Plastic flowers and beads add an unexpected pop of texture and color. The finished piece is stapled onto a readymade canvas.

## Materials

- Pattern pieces on page 116 (do not add seam allowances)
- 5" × 7" (12.5cm × 18cm) canvas on a wooden frame
- 8" × 10" (20.5cm × 25.5cm) piece of printed cotton fabric for background
- 8" × 10" (20.5cm × 25.5cm) piece of fusible fleece for padding
- Fusible interfacing
- Assorted felt scraps in yellow, red, brown, tan, orange, green for mushroom caps, leaves
- Printed cotton scraps in brown, white, yellow for mushroom stems
- Sewing threads in white, yellow, orange, green
- Plastic flowers and beads

## Tools

- Iron
- Marking pen
- Sewing machine
- Sewing needle
- Staple gun
- Scissors

**Dimensions**
5 1/4" × 7 1/4" (13.5cm × 18.5cm)

**1** Follow the package directions to iron the fusible fleece to the underside of the fabric. Turn the fabric right side up and center the canvas on the fabric. You should have 1 ½" (4cm) of additional fabric on all four sides. Mark the corners of the canvas with four pins to mark the boundaries of the image area, and set the canvas aside.

**2** Thread the sewing machine with white thread and make a series of individual wavy seams to resemble grass. Each stem should begin at the base of the image area and end before the top pin marks. Switch to green thread and make additional darker stems (Fig. 1). If you are more comfortable stitching over drawn lines, use a marking pen to draw the design with marking pen first, and then stitch over the lines.

**3** Iron fusible interfacing to the underside of the fabric scraps, then cut out the stem shapes; do not add a seam allowance. Cut out the coordinating felt mushroom caps. Pin the stems and caps to the fabric, placing them over the stitched grass seams (Fig. 2). Working with one stem at a time, remove the pin and paper backing and iron the stem in place. Continue working in this fashion until all the stems are ironed in place.

**4** Move back to the sewing machine and stitch around the inside edge of each mushroom stem. Alternate between using a straight seam around the inside edge of some of the stems or spanning a tight, small zigzag seam around the outside edge of the other stems. Use a straight seam just inside the outside edge to attach the mushroom caps. Refer to the pattern to make one or two decorative darts along the bottom edge. You may consider changing thread colors and making a second or third decorative seam.

**Fig. 1**

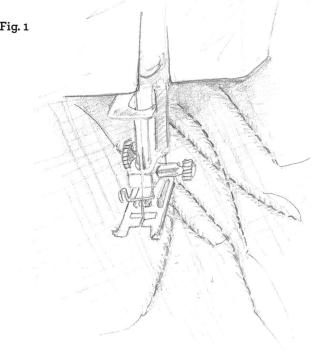

**Fig. 2**

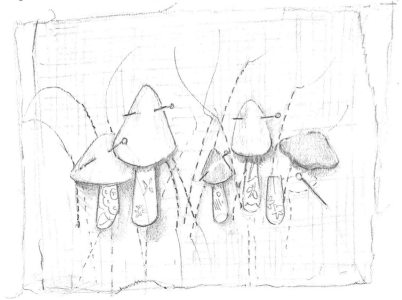

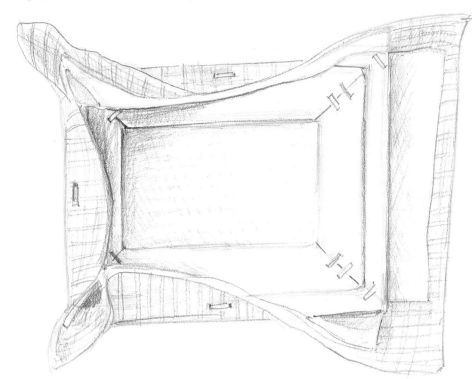

**Fig. 3**

## TIP

Staple gunning the finished piece to the canvas is easier with a second set of hands. Have someone hold the fabric while you pull the trigger.

If you're unhappy with the appearance of a fold or a staple, use a flathead screwdriver to pull up the staple and redo.

**5** Cut five felt leaves and arrange them alongside the dark green grass stems and pin them in place. Thread the sewing machine with green thread and machine stitch the center of each leaf in place with a small straight seam.

**6** Use a sewing needle to pull the top threads to the underside of the work. Tie each pair of threads into a knot and trim the threads.

**7** Arrange the plastic flowers and beads at the end of some of the grass stems and around the mushrooms. Try to distribute the colors and sizes around your design. To sew them on, thread the needle with white thread and knot the end.

Poke the needle up from the underside and then string a flower followed by a round bead onto the needle. Poke the needle back down through the flower. The bead will hold it in place. Repeat the stitch a second time for reinforcement, then knot and trim the ends. Continue working this way to attach the remaining flower and bead sets.

**8** Turn the finished piece over and pull up the fleece at the corners. Use scissors to cut out a 1½" (4cm) square at each corner. This will eliminate bulk at the corners.

Place the canvas facedown in the center of the fabric piece. Pull the fabric up over the edges so it lies flat against the back of the wood frame. Fire the staple through the fabric, fleece and into the wood. Place the first four staples in the center of each side (Fig. 3). To fold the corners, tuck one half of the fabric under the other to make a fold line and then wrap it around the edge of the frame. Trap all the layers in the staple. Repeat the process to make three more clean corners. Place eight additional staples along the edges to ensure that the fabric is pulled tight in all directions. Trim the fabric edges to give the piece a professional finish.

# Flower Canvas

There's nothing like a bright bouquet of everlasting flowers to uplift your décor and put you in a sunny mood. Growing a fabric garden has never been easier!

## Materials

- ⮑ 8" × 10" (20.5cm × 25.5cm) canvas on wooden frame
- ⮑ 11" × 13" (28cm × 33cm) piece of printed cotton fabric for background
- ⮑ 11" × 13" (28cm × 33cm) piece of fusible fleece for padding
- ⮑ Printed cotton in pink, red for flowers
- ⮑ Fusible interfacing
- ⮑ Plastic flower and round beads
- ⮑ Felt scraps in pink, red, orange, yellow, green for flowers, leaves
- ⮑ Thread in light and dark green, orange

## Tools

- ⮑ Iron
- ⮑ Marking pen
- ⮑ Sewing machine
- ⮑ Sewing needle
- ⮑ Staple gun
- ⮑ Scissors
- ⮑ Die cut machine with flower dies in various sizes
- ⮑ Straight pins

**Dimensions**

8" × 10" (20.5cm × 25.5cm)

## Flower Canvas Instructions

*Prepare the fabric and make stems as indicated in steps 1-2 of Mushroom Canvas (page 51). Stop some of the stem seams halfway to punctuate them with rounded leaves. Use the die cut machine to cut the flowers out of the felt scraps and arrange the felt flowers on your canvas and pin them in place. Decide which flowers would benefit from the addition of pattern fabric circles and fuse them either on top or under the felt flowers. Machine stitch the flowers with fabric in place with zigzag edging or freestyle loops using the orange thread. The remaining flower centers are sewn in place with the plastic flowers and beads. Arrange the felt leaves over the design, pin them in place and use the green threads to machine stitch around the inside edge. Staple to canvas frame as indicated in step 8 of Mushroom Canvas (page 52).*

# tabletop trees

These whimsical trees will brighten your home during the holidays and throughout the new year. Alternate panels of felt and fabric are sewn together to make either the evergreen or drop-shaped tree. The stuffed tree is embellished with layered felt circles and buttons. The dowel rod trunk slides up the base of the finished tree and is anchored in a drilled section of branch.

## Materials

- ➲ Pattern pieces on page 116
- ➲ Fat quarter each of two complementary patterned cottons
- ➲ Fat quarter each of green and dark green felt
- ➲ Assorted felt scraps in white, light blue, various greens for circles
- ➲ Sewing thread
- ➲ Embroidery floss in assorted greens
- ➲ Fiberfill stuffing
- ➲ Buttons in assorted greens and whites
- ➲ 2 green felt beads, small and large
- ➲ 13" (33cm) length of ½" (1.5cm) wide dowel rod – 12" (30.5cm) length for the tear drop variation
- ➲ 2" × 2" (5cm × 5cm) section of branch drilled with a ½" (1.5cm) diameter × 1" (2.5cm) deep center hole

*Note: If you don't have access to a tree branch, you can substitute round or square wood plaques or set the base of the rods into plaster-filled plant pots.

## Tools

- ➲ Die cut machine and templates for ³/₄" (2cm), 1 ¼" (3cm) and 1 ³/₄" (4.5cm) size circles
- ➲ Scissors
- ➲ Straight pins
- ➲ Crewel needle
- ➲ Sewing needle
- ➲ Sewing machine
- ➲ Glue gun and melt sticks

**Dimensions**
15" (38cm) tall

**1** Cut two Evergreen Tree Shapes out of each of the felts and fabrics. Placing right sides together, pair each fabric piece with a felt piece. Pin and stitch a straight seam down the flat edge. You'll have four sides when you're finished (Fig. 1).

**2** Pin the four sides right sides together. Connect a felt piece to a fabric piece. They should alternate all the way around (Fig. 2).

**3** Begin stitching the sides together. Start your seam at the top of the tree and align the presser foot along the cut edge going in and out of the points (see Turning a Corner on page 15). Leave the flat edge at the base of the tree unsewn. Repeat the process to connect the three remaining sides; this create a hollow center that will be stuffed later. Clip the excess felt and fabric off the points of the branches (Fig. 3).

**4** Cut the Tree Base piece out of felt, fold it in half and clip a small x-shaped opening in the center (Fig. 4). Position the base piece at the bottom of the tree and line up your pointed branches at each corner of the square base. Pin the felt to the flat bottom edge of the tree sides. Make three separate seams to machine stitch each side together, leave the fourth side unsewn and turn the tree right side out. I found a stuffing stick/knitting needle helpful to turn the pointed branches right side out.

**5** Stuff the top of the tree and the points first. Then fill the rest of the tree. Arrange the felt circles and buttons primarily over the felt sections of the tree. Position the larger circles and buttons around the bottom half of the tree using straight pins to hold them in place. String a crewel needle with a full strand of floss and insert the needle under an edge of a felt circle to hide your knots. Pull the needle out through the buttons. After stitching the button in place, make a series of decorative straight stitches around the contour of the felt circle. You can either tie the end in a knot under the felt or draw the needle across the inside of the tree to the next cluster of circles and buttons. I sometimes attach buttons in one color and make the decorative stitches in another.

Fig. 1

Fig. 2

Fig. 3

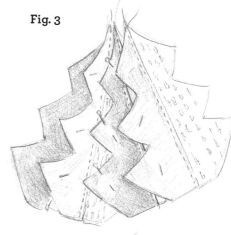

Fig. 4

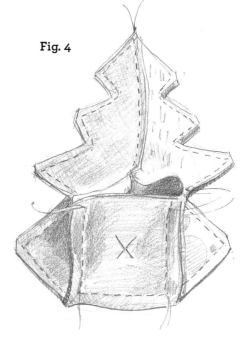

**6** Switch to a sewing needle and thread to stitch together the very top of the tree. Poke in any frayed edges and make small invisible stitches to close up the opening. While the thread is still connected, draw the needle up through a button and two felt beads to make a decorative cap. Bring the

needle back down through all three pieces and repeat the process until the decorations are stable before knotting and trimming the thread.

**7** Anchor dowel rod into the base, if necessary stabilize with wood or craft glue and let it dry before inserting it into the

tree. Once set insert the open dowel rod end through the notched opening until the end sits right under the decorative cap. Hand stitch the opening closed at the base. To stop the dowel rod from slipping out squeeze a little hot glue onto the connection of the dowel to the notched fabric.

# Tear Drop Tree

This is slightly easier to make than the evergeen tree because each panel is a single piece.

### Tear Drop Tree Instructions

*Using the Tear Drop Base, cut two pattern pieces each from the felt and fabric. Skip step 1. For quick way to embellish the tree, use fusible interfacing instead of stitching to attach the circle embellishments. Follow the manufacturer's directions to back the circles and fuse them to the inside portion of the felt teardrop shapes. Continue assembling the tree following steps 2-7 on pages 56-57, skipping step 5 if you used the fusible interfacing. Use embroidery floss to embellish the tree as desired.*

## Materials

- Pattern pieces on page 116
- Fat quarter of patterned cotton with complementary colors
- Fat quarter of green felt
- Assorted scraps of white, light blue, various greens for circles
- Sewing thread
- Embroidery floss in assorted greens
- Fiberfill stuffing
- Buttons in assorted greens, blues
- 2 felt beads, large green, small blue
- 12" (30.5cm) length of ½" (1.5cm) dowel
- 2" × 2" (5cm x 5cm) section of branch drilled with a ½" (1.5cm) diameter × 1" (2.5cm) deep center hole
- Fusible interfacing

## Tools

- Die cut machine and templates for ¾" (2cm), 1 ¼" (3cm) and 1 ¾" (4.5cm) size circles
- Scissors
- Straight pins
- Crewel needle
- Sewing needle
- Sewing machine
- Glue gun and melt sticks
- Iron

### Dimensions
*13½" (34.5cm) tall*

# standing deer

Deer in the wild captivate me. Their quiet beauty is breath taking. I'm drawn to the stylized wildlife imagery in early Disney movies and the wonderful vintage deer crafts from the '60s. Drawing all these visual cues together, I designed a pair of standing deer that would love to roam a tabletop tree forest.

## Materials

### Buck

- Pattern pieces on page 117
- ¼ yard 100% wool felt in ochre for belly, antlers, tail
- Fiberfill
- 3 chenille stems
- ¼ yard 35% wool felt in medium brown for body, tail, ear
- Two 6mm safety eyes
- Scrap of light beige felt for eye
- Brown pom-poms
- Thread

### Doe

- Use all the same materials and tools listed above but do not use the Antler pattern pieces and switch the felt colors to:
- ¼ yard of 100% ochre felt for body, tail, ears
- ¼ yard 35% wool felt in light beige for belly, tail, ears
- Scrap of 100% wool felt in white for eyes

Note: The doe's body is made of 100% wool felt so you could easily adapt her into a fawn by needle felting spots directly onto her back.

## Tools

- Sewing machine
- Sewing needle
- Straight pins
- Scissors
- Wire cutters
- Hot glue gun and melt sticks

### Dimensions

8 ½" (21.5cm) (11" [28cm] with antlers) × 6 ½" (16.5cm)

**1** Cut four Antler pieces and two Underside pieces out of 100% ochre wool felt. Pin each pair of antlers together and machine stitch around the outside edge, leaving the bottom open. Use the wire cutters to cut two 3" (7.5cm) sections of chenille stem, and insert one into each stitched antler. Pin the Underside pieces together and connect them with a single straight seam along the top (Fig. 1).

**2** Cut two Body pieces and one Back of Head piece out of medium brown felt.

Placing right sides together, position one of the antlers topside down onto the Top of Head piece. Align the Top of Head piece with the nose mark on the Body piece. Pin the antler over the Top of Head and along the back of the neck on the Body piece, trapping the end of the antlers between the layers (Fig. 2). Machine stitch the piece in place. Your machine shouldn't have any trouble sewing over the chenille stem end.

**3** Repeat with the remaining antler and Body piece; be sure the antlers and body pieces are properly aligned and pinned before sewing the layers together (Fig. 3).

**4** Position the Underside piece up under the legs of the Body pieces, right sides together. Align the legs and pin the edges together. Pin the chest up against the body pieces. Beginning at the chest, make a seam that connects one side of the Underside to one side of the Body. Work your way up and down around both legs, ending the seam at his backside.

Repeat the process on the other side of the Underside to the other side of the Body.

**5** Flatten the deer and make two more seams to connect the body pieces together. One seam spans from the nose to the chest. The second seam spans the back of the neck across the back, leaving an opening at the backside to turn the deer right side out (Fig. 4). Check all your seams on both sides and turn the deer right side out. Carefully push the hoof-end up into the leg until you can easily pull it free.

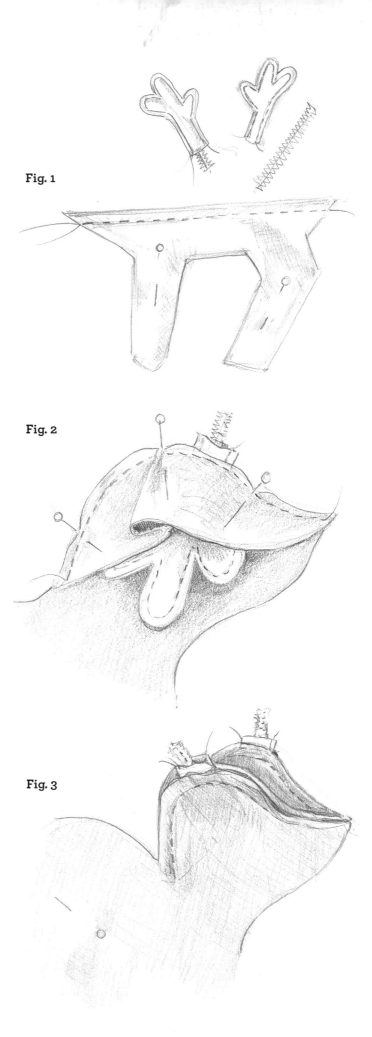

Fig. 1

Fig. 2

Fig. 3

**Fig. 4**          **Fig. 5**

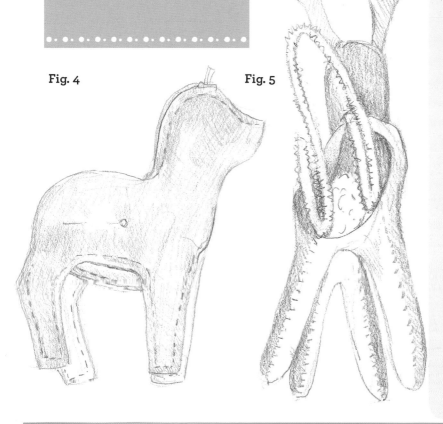

**6** Cut two eye shapes out of ochre felt and attach the safety eyes, positioning the felt eyes over the opening you create in the head (see *Adding Safety Eyes* on page 16).

Stuff the head and ends of the hooves, pushing the stuffing in place. Fold a chenille stem in half, then turn each end up a ½" (1.5cm). Insert the chenille stem ends into the front legs (Fig. 5). Finish stuffing the legs and neck. Repeat the process with the second chenille stem inserting it into the back legs before completing the stuffing.

**7** Cut a pair of Ear pieces out of both medium brown and ochre, and a Tail piece out of brown and light beige. Stack the two different colored ears and tailpieces together, then stitch around the edges, leaving the bottom open to turn them right side out. Fold the base of the Ear pieces in half and stitch them to the sides of the deer's head. Insert the end of the Tail piece in the opening in the deer's backside and stitch it in place while you hand stitch the opening closed. Hot glue a pom-pom to the end of the nose.

Repeat steps 1–7 for the doe, omitting the antler pieces.

# Garland

This clever technique can be used on any sized felt circle or shape. It lends itself to decorating a mantle, window or tree. Use felted sweater fabric and more reinforcing seams to adapt the design to make yourself a scarf!

## Materials

- ➲ 35% wool felt in pink, mauve, light blue, dark blue, green, red
- ➲ Thread

## Tools

- ➲ Die cut machine with ¾" (2cm), 1¼" (3cm), 1½" (4cm) circle templates
- ➲ Sewing machine

### Garland Instructions

*Position the edge of a felt circle under your presser foot. Begin stitching straight across the circle ending ⅛" (3mm) before the edge. Set the needle and lift the presser foot. Position the edge of a second circle over the end of the first circle. Continue the seam, inserting circles as you stitch. When you're stitching across the larger circles, stop to insert a small decorative circle. Be careful to distribute colors, sizes and overlapping combinations down the length of the garland. Reinforce the seam by backstitching before cutting the thread.*

# fanciful houses

Magical felt and fabric homes for dolls and fairies—these will add whimsy to any décor. The felt sides have window and door openings cut into them. Each opening is backed with a printed fabric and then machine stitched in place. An inner cardboard sleeve adds stability to the stuffed structure. Make one or a whole village. To take the whimsy with you, skip the cardboard and stuffing, and line the house with felt to make a playful tote.

## Materials to Make Both Houses

- ➲ ½ yard 35% wool felt in white for house sides, roof base
- ➲ 100% wool felt in putty for shutters
- ➲ 35% wool felt in green for shrubberies
- ➲ ⅛ yard total 35% wool felt in assorted colors including blue turquoise, orange red, pink for roof shingles, window boxes, doors
- ➲ 4" × 5" (10cm × 12.5cm) orange felt for large house base piece
- ➲ 3" × 4 ¼" (7.5cm × 11cm) turquoise felt for small house base piece
- ➲ Assorted printed cotton to back door and window openings
- ➲ Miniature felt flowers, butterflies
- ➲ Two Styrofoam bricks
- ➲ Fiberfill
- ➲ Posterboard
- ➲ Packing tape
- ➲ Embroidery floss in green, turquoise, pink
- ➲ Two ¼" (6mm) tan two-hole buttons for door knobs
- ➲ Sewing thread

## Tools

- ➲ Sewing machine
- ➲ Sewing needle
- ➲ Crewel needle
- ➲ Straight pins
- ➲ Scissors
- ➲ Stapler
- ➲ Die cutting machine with 1 ¼" (3cm) and 1" (2.5cm) circle templates

### Dimensions

*Little house: 9" × 4 ¾" × 5" (23cm × 12cm × 12.5cm)*

*Big house: 10 ½" × 6 ½" × 6" (26.5cm × 16.5cm × 15cm)*

Fig. 1

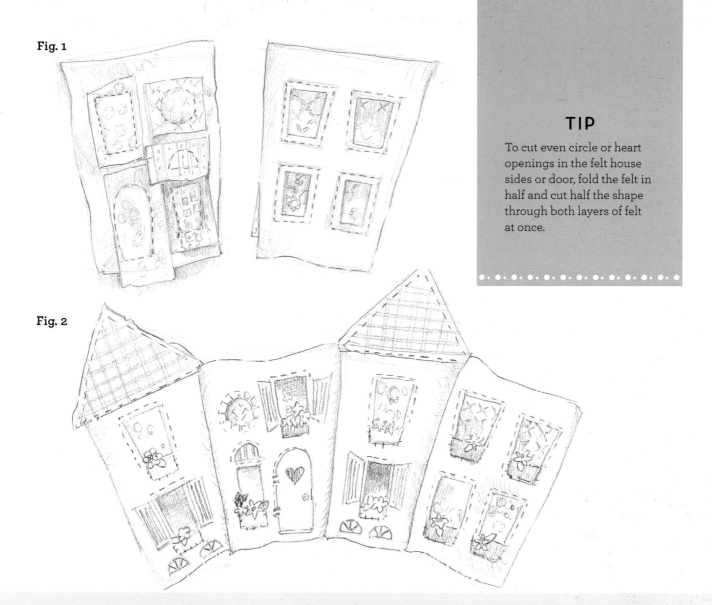

Fig. 2

**TIP**

To cut even circle or heart openings in the felt house sides or door, fold the felt in half and cut half the shape through both layers of felt at once.

**1**

Make one house at a time. Use the templates to cut two Side pieces and two Front and Back pieces from white felt. Cut an 8" × 7" (21cm × 18.5cm) base roof piece out of white felt (8" × 5" [21cm × 12.5cm] for the small house). Mark the openings and cut out the windows and doors (for the Back pieces, omit the door opening and mark the windows where desired).

**2**

Cut sections of printed fabric to place behind each window and door opening. Make sure the fabric is at least ¼" (6mm) wider and longer than each opening. Position the fabric behind the openings and pin them in place. Working on the right side of the house, machine stitch around each of the openings to connect the fabric (Fig. 1). Cut triangles of printed fabric to place over the gabled tops of the house sides. Fold and press under ¼" (6mm) of the bottom straight fabric edge, then pin and topstitch it in place.

**3**

Placing the pieces right sides together, line up the edge of the house front with a house side. Machine stitch a single straight seam to join them together. Next, attach the open side of the house to the house back. Repeat the process until just one corner of the four house pieces remains unattached. All four pieces will be connected, but the house will still be flat (Fig. 2).

**4**

Free cut the shutters out of putty colored felt, then cut the window boxes, green leaves and a door out of the colored felt scraps. Use the crewel needle threaded with a full strand of colored floss to attach a shutter to each side of the windows with three

63

long decorative stitches. Switch to green floss to attach the felt circle shrubberies under or beside the windows on the sides of the house. Make four elongated cross-stitches that intersect in the middle of each circle. To fit a bush under a window, cut the circle in half and shorten the stitches to make smaller diagonal stitches. Attach the door to one side of the opening with two sets of small stitches that look like hinges.

**5** Using a sewing needle, hand stitch a window box under a window. After attaching a window box, bring the needle up under the window and string it with the following sequence: felt leaf, felt flower, sequin, bead. Poke the needle back down through the sequin, felt flower and leaf. The bead will hold the stitch in place. Repeat the process to attach multiple flowers to the top of each window box. Use the sewing needle and thread to stitch a small button doorknob to the front and back of the door.

**6** Cut 1 1/2" (4cm) wide strips of either irregular, curvy or squared shingles out of the colored felt. I used cool colors (blue, turquoise and purple) for the small house, and warm colors (pink, red and orange) for the big house. Cut each strip longer than the width of the roof. They'll be trimmed after they're sewn in place. Cut a 3" (7.5cm) wide center top piece, with decorative cuts on either side.

Starting on the edge of the roof, lay a strip so it hangs over the bottom edge of the white

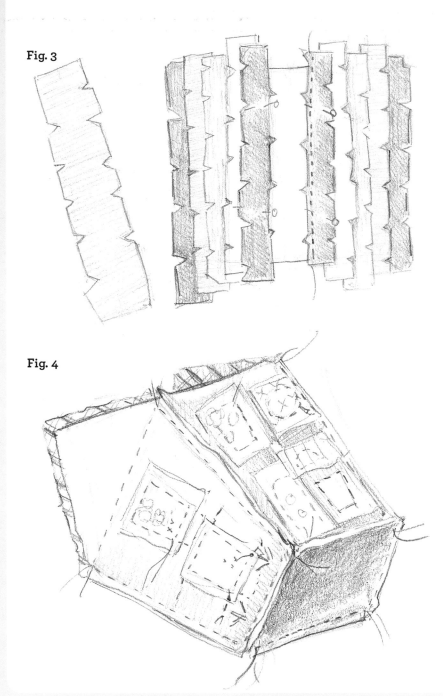

Fig. 3

Fig. 4

roof piece. Machine stitch the straight inside strip edge in place (Fig. 3). Repeat the process on the other side of the roof. Overlap the second strip over the straight edge of the first strip and then machine stitch the straight edge in place. Repeat the process to add the second strip to the other side of the roof.

Continue working this way, covering the roof in shingles.

Finish by sewing the center of the wide top piece to the roof ridge. Turn the finished roof wrong side up and trim the strip edges so they overhang the white felt by 1/4" (6mm).

**7** Placing right sides together, pin the open edge of the house front with the open side. Machine stitch them together. Place the base piece over the bottom of the house. Pin the

# People

Create some people to live in your felt and fabric village. Make one for each member of the family!

## Materials

- ➲ Miniature wooden doll family
- ➲ Acrylic paint
- ➲ Small paintbrush
- ➲ Water cup
- ➲ Paper towel
- ➲ Protected surface

### People Instructions

*Paint simple clothes, hair and two eyes onto each of the wooden shapes. It's important to dry your brush after dipping it in the water, as watery paint drips. Allow the base clothes color to dry before adding accessories like ties or decorative accents.*

**Fig. 5**

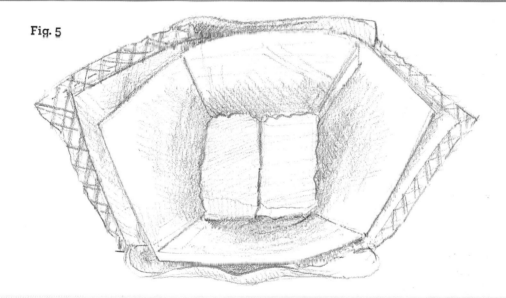

8  edges together and machine stitch it in place (Fig. 4). Trim the corners and turn the house right side out.

Trace the Front and Back and Side pattern pieces onto the posterboard, lining up the long edges. Cut out a single connected piece (the basic shape will look like Fig. 2), fold the connections and test fit the cardboard inside the felt house

before sealing the open side closed with packing tape. You'll also need to cut a posterboard roof and base piece, and score the ridgeline of the roof. Place the posterboard base pieces inside the felt house (Fig. 5). Pull the fabric edges of the front and back portions of the house up and over the posterboard and staple them to the center of each edge. Insert the Styrofoam brick and

fill between the felt house and bricks with fiberfill stuffing.

9  Hand stitch one side of the edge of the white felt roof base to the top of the house. Fill the roof with additional fiberfill and insert the posterboard roof between the felt and the fiberfill. Hand stitch the other side of the roof in place.

# lovable plushies

It's incredibly rewarding to sew up a creation that everyone wants to pick up, hug and take home. The projects in this chapter are especially lovable—the *Hilarious Hoots* on page 84 and *Happy Hedgehogs* on page 68 are some of my most popular designs.

If this is your first time making plushies, you're in for a treat. Much easier to stitch than clothing, these fabric friends are made up by stitching pattern pieces right sides together. Then the assembled piece is turned right side out. Your creation begins to take shape when it's stuffed with soft fiberfill.

The mixture of different textured fabrics and colors creates stuffed animals that beg to be loved and hugged. The hedgehogs have plush fur and fleece bodies with felt accents and accessories. I picked a vintage-inspired pairing of plush felt and mini print cotton to stitch together the *Kitty and Dachshund* on page 72. Simple embroidery and button eyes bring their stuffed bodies to life.

Both the *Snappy Turtle* on page 76 and *Hilarious Hoots* on page 84 integrate fleece, fabric and felt. The *Summer Friends* set on page 80 set beautifully blends felt and fabric together. The 100% wool felt heads allow you to effortlessly needle felt features onto the doll's faces.

Make plushies for all the kids in your life, both young and old!

# happy hedgehogs

No one can resist this sweet softie pair. Their rounded backs are a comfort to hug while their sleepy eyes gaze up with love. Sewn together with durable fleece and plush fun fur, felt plays a vital role in all the embellishments—ears, eyelids, nose, flowers and base.

## Materials for One Hedgehog

- ➲ Pattern pieces on page 120
- ➲ 1/3 yard off-white fleece
- ➲ Small scrap of 35% wool felt in light brown for eyelids
- ➲ Embroidery floss in light brown
- ➲ 1/3 yard plush fur
- ➲ Fiberfill stuffing
- ➲ White thread
- ➲ Felt beads
- ➲ Felt flowers (you can cut your own)
- ➲ 8mm brown safety eyes

### Scarf

- ➲ Two 1" × 7" (2.5cm × 18cm) pieces of pink felt
- ➲ Two 3/4" × 7" (2cm × 18cm) pieces of red felt
- ➲ 3 1/2" × 28" (9cm × 71cm) piece of purple felt

## Tools

- ➲ Crewel needle
- ➲ Sewing needle
- ➲ Sewing machine
- ➲ Scissors
- ➲ Straight pins
- ➲ Pinking shears

**Dimensions**
*11" × 7" (28cm × 18cm)*

**Fig. 1**

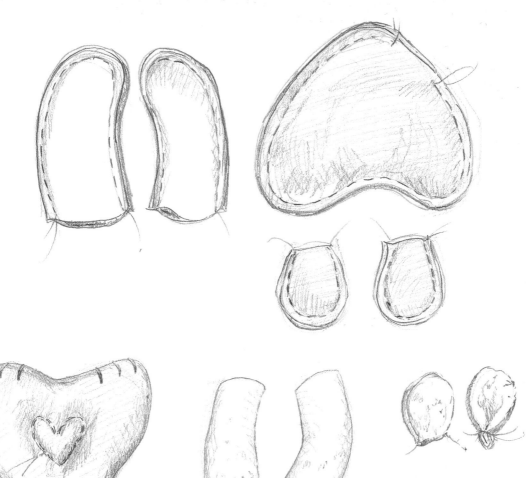

**Fig. 2**

**1** Cut four Arm pieces out of fleece. Cut four Ear pieces, two from fleece and two from felt. Cut two Feet pieces, one from fleece and one from felt.

Pin and stitch each pair of arms together. Leave the base open.

Placing right sides together, pin a felt ear over a fleece ear. Stitch around the outside edge, leaving the base open. Repeat to make the second ear.

Placing right sides together, stack the felt Feet piece over the fleece Feet piece. Stitch around the outside edge, leaving the marked opening unstitched. (Fig. 1).

**2** Turn all the pieces in step 1 right side out and lightly stuff them.

Place the center of the feet back in the machine and stitch a heart through both layers. String a crewel needle with a full thickness of embroidery thread. Insert the needle in through the opening and draw it out through the fleece side of one side of the foot piece. Make three toe stitches on each side of the feet. When you're finished, knot the thread on the fleece side of each foot. It will be hidden when the feet are attached.

Rethread the needle with another strand of floss. Insert the needle into the opening in the arm and draw it out through the hand. Make three stitches, bring the thread back out, and knot it at the opening. Repeat the process to make three stitches in the other hand.

Pinch the unsewn edge of an ear, and then place it in the machine to stitch across the gather (Fig. 2).

**3** Cut two body pieces out of fleece. Position and pin an ear and arm to each body piece. Machine stitch them in place (Fig. 3). Pin the end of each arm to the stomach to keep it out of the way while the back pieces are attached.

**4** Cut two back of the body pieces out of plush fur. Position each one right side down over a body piece. Pin the fur to the outside edge of the fleece body. Machine stitch the fur to the fleece. Check the connections of the ears and arms and then make a second seam to reinforce the connection (Fig. 4). Unpin the arms from the belly and re-pin them to the fur back to keep them out of the way for the next step.

**5** Place the body pieces right sides together, being sure to line the nose and fur connections, then pin the edges. Make a continuous seam around the entire outside of the hedgehog, leaving an opening at the base of the fur back. Make a second reinforcing seam before turning the piece right side out.

Partially stuff the nose and face. Clip a small opening on the side of the face, approximately 1" (2.5cm) down from the ear. Insert the safety eye through the opening. Reach inside the opening at the base of the hedgehog and thread the backing onto the eye. Repeat the process to attach the second eye. Place additional stuffing in the head to fill out the face. This will help you stitch the mouth.

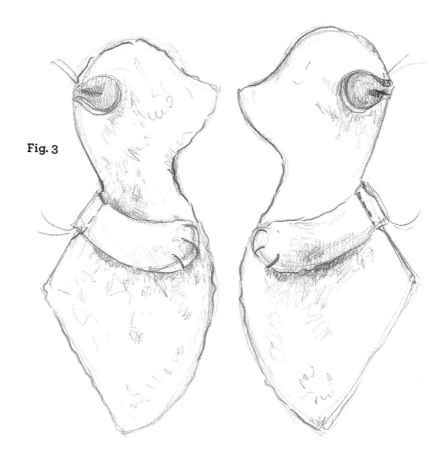

**Fig. 3**

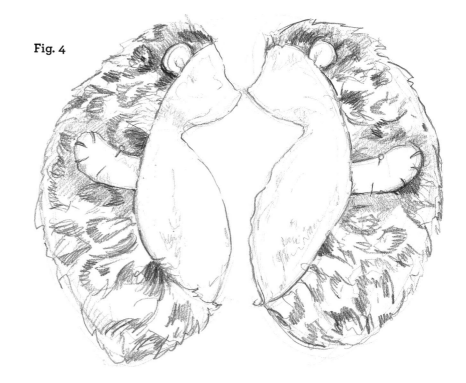

**Fig. 4**

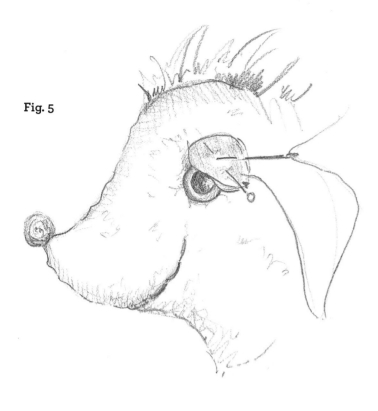

**Fig. 5**

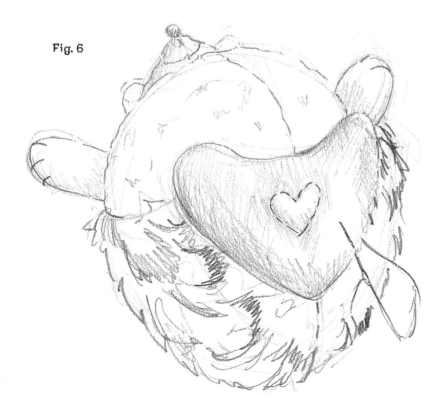

**Fig. 6**

To make the mouth, string a crewel needle with a full strand of floss. Insert the needle up through the opening and out through the face 1" (2.5cm) down from the eye. Make three connected stitches to form a half smile. Complete the smile by making three more stitches that curve up the other side of the face. Bring the needle out through the fur behind the ear, and tie the floss in a knot.

Cut a 1" (2.5cm) diameter circle out of two eyelids out of the light brown felt. Cut the circle in half. Place one half over the top half of the eye and hand stitch it in place (Fig. 5). Draw the needle across the inside of the head to attach the other half of the circle to the other eye. Use the remaining thread to stitch the felt bead to the end of the nose, and the flowers behind the ear.

**6** Continue stuffing the entire body. Hand stitch the plush fur opening closed. Place more stuffing inside the feet and hand stitch it to the base of the finished hedgehog (Fig. 6). I was able to tuck in the fabric from the opening and stitch it closed while connecting the feet in place.

**7** To make the purple felt scarf, use pinking shears to trim both sides of the pink and red felt. Wrap pink felt strips around each end of the scarf and pin them in place. Machine stitch a single seam on both ends of the scarf to attach both sides of the strips to the scarf. Wrap a red felt strip around the center of each of the pink strips and machine stitch them in place.

# kitty and dachshund

After a hilarious visit with my sister's dog, I was inspired to design a dachshund plushie. After the pattern was underway I stumbled across the cover of a vintage *McCall's* 1953 pattern that featured a sleepy kitten. My neighbor stopped over while I was struggling to update the cat design. In an amazing coincidence, her aunt had sewn the exact toys from the pattern and she had saved them. I was thrilled to hold the originals in my hands, and from then on both designs fell into place.

## Kitty Materials

- Pattern pieces on page 121-122
- $1/3$ yard caramel plush felt for body, head, tail, ears
- $1/4$ yard pink vintage-inspired cotton print for belly, ears
- Scrap of 100% wool felt in putty
- $7/8$" (2cm) wide plaid ribbon
- Fiberfill stuffing
- Embroidery floss in pink, brown
- Two $5/8$" (1cm) brown shank buttons
- Sewing thread
- Ribbon

## Tools

- Sewing machine
- Crewel needle
- Sewing needle
- Straight pins
- Scissors
- Stuffing stick or knitting needle

### Dimensions

*Nose to rump 9 1/2" (24cm), 7" (18cm) high, 8" (20.5cm) wide at back legs*

## Kitty

This adorable kitty is perfectly sized to fit in a child's arms, and flat enough to snuggle in for the night. Plush felt is a delight to stitch, and it doesn't shed like fun fur equivalents. Plush felt is lighter weight than conventional fun furs, which enables it to integrate easily with thin, vintage-inspired cotton prints. If you're sewing a kitty for a very young child, please switch the button eyes for embroidered or safety eyes.

**Fig. 1**

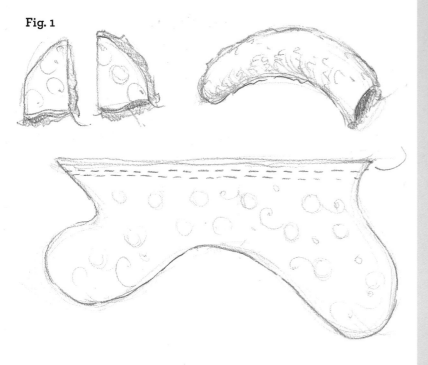

**Fig. 2**

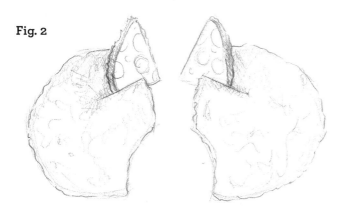

**Fig. 3**

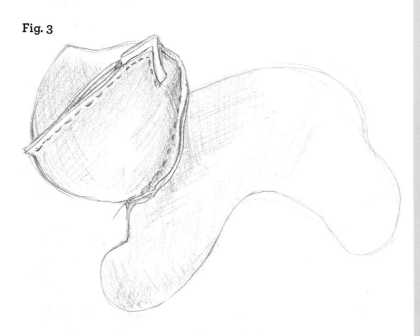

**1** Cut two Kitty Underside pieces out of cotton. Place them right sides together, pin them, and make a straight seam across the top. Cut a pair of Kitty Ear pieces out of cotton and plush felt. Placing right sides together, stack a cotton ear over a plush ear. Pin them together and then stitch around the outside edge of each ear. Leave the bottom edge open and turn the ears right side out. Repeat for the second ear.

Cut two Kitty Tail pieces out of plush felt. Stack them right sides together, pin them, and stitch around the outside edge. Leave the bottom edge unsewn and turn the tail right side out (Fig. 1). Use a stuffing stick to push fiberfill into the tip of the tail. Continue stuffing, leaving the last 1" (2.5cm) unstuffed.

**2** Cut two Kitty Side of Head pieces out of plush felt. Cut into the Side of Head pieces where marked on the pattern. Insert the rounded side of the ear into the slit (Fig. 2). Fold the headpiece, right sides together, along the slit line, lining up the bottom flat edge of the ear with the edges of the slit. Machine stitch along the slit, trapping the bottom edge of the ear in your seam.

**3** Cut two Kitty Body pieces and a single Kitty Top of Head piece out of the plush felt. Placing right sides together, stitch each neck section of the Top of Head piece to the Body pieces. Position the nose of the Top of Head piece between the nose of the Side of Head pieces (Fig. 3).

Continue pinning the Top of Head to the top of the Side of Head. Fold the other ear forward and be sure to trap it between the Top of Head piece and the Side of Head piece. Machine stitch in place. Repeat the pinning and stitching process to connect the Top of Head and Side of Head into one complete head piece, this time stitching from the nose to the neck.

**4** Position the cotton Kitty Underside right sides together with underside of the cat body pieces. Align and pin each cotton

**Fig. 4**

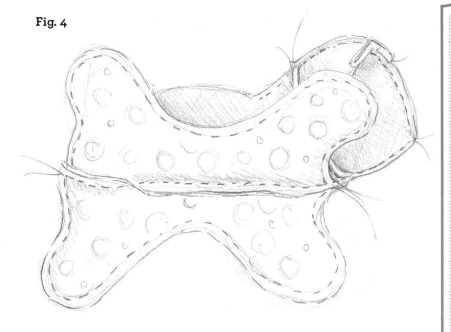

**Fig. 5**

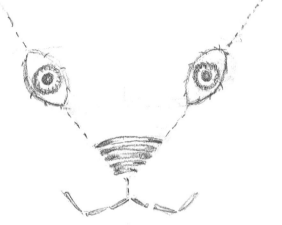

# Dachshund

*This playful pup is just as squishy and lovable as the kitty. He features a vintage blue cowboy print on his tummy and ears and is simpler to make than the kitty. Skip step 2—the end of his ears fit flat between the side of the head and top of the headpieces in step 3.*

## Dachshund Materials

- ➲ Pattern pieces on pages 121-122
- ➲ ⅓ yard brown plush felt
- ➲ ¼ yard blue vintage-inspired cotton print
- ➲ Scrap of caramel colored plush felt for the eyes
- ➲ ⅞" (2cm) wide plaid ribbon
- ➲ Fiberfill stuffing
- ➲ Embroidery floss in ochre, brown
- ➲ Two ⅜" (1cm) brown shank buttons
- ➲ Sewing thread
- ➲ Ribbon

## Tools

- ➲ Sewing machine
- ➲ Crewel needle
- ➲ Sewing needle
- ➲ Straight pins
- ➲ Scissors

### Dimensions

*Nose to rump 14" (35.5cm), 9 ½" (24cm) high, 10" (25.5cm) wide at back legs*

leg over a plush leg. Fit and pin the pointed chest where the head and neck pieces meet. Start the seam at this point and machine stitch from the neck around both legs. End at the backside. Repeat the process on the other side to connect the other half of the underside (Fig. 4).

**5** Pin the back of the Body pieces together and machine stitch from the base of the neck across the back, leaving an opening where indicated on the pattern. Turn the kitty right side out.

Partially stuff the head to help position the facial features. Thread a full strand of pink floss through the crewel needle. Insert the needle through the opening and draw it out at the nose. Create a satin stitch nose (see Satin Stitch on page 17). Reach inside to tie the end in a knot. Switch to a full strand of brown floss to stitch an upturned mouth.

Switch to a sewing needle and thread. Cut two small oval shapes from the putty felt. Determine the placement of the eyes along the seams on each side of the face; layer a button over the felt oval eye, and stitch them in that spot. Repeat this to add the second eye to the other side of the face (Fig. 5).

Stuff the rest of the head, legs, neck and body. Insert the tail into the opening and hand stitch the opening closed while trapping the tail in place.

Tie on the ribbon bow, and, meow, your kitty is done!

# snappy turtle

Turtle shells lend themselves to felt and fabric decorations. The printed dot cotton fabric and appliqué felt circles combine to make a dynamic shell. I struggled with how to decorate the edge of the shell until I remembered how pom-pom trim had been incorporated into softie designs in the 1960s. This fellow is constructed in three separate parts: a top shell, body, and chest piece. His arms, legs and tail can tuck inside the chest piece.

## Materials

- Pattern pieces on pages 122-123
- ¼ yard pink fleece for top shell
- ½ yard orange fleece for underside of shell
- Spotted printed cotton for shell rim
- 27" (68.5cm) pom-pom trim
- Fiberfill stuffing
- ½ yard green fleece for turtle body
- ¼ yard yellow fleece for chest
- ¼ yard dark green felt for chest
- 35% wool felt scraps in various greens, dark and light orange, bright and light pink, yellow, white for spots
- Embroidery floss in pink
- Two ½" (1.5cm) black shank buttons
- ¼ yard 35% wool in dark green for chest, spots
- Sewing thread

## Tools

- Sewing machine
- Sewing needle
- Straight pins
- Scissors

**Dimensions**

15" (38cm) long, 9 ½" (24cm) tall and 9 ⅓" (23.5cm) wide

**Fig. 1**

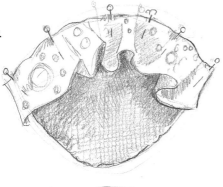

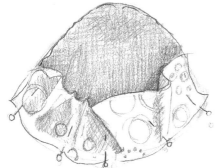

**Fig. 2**

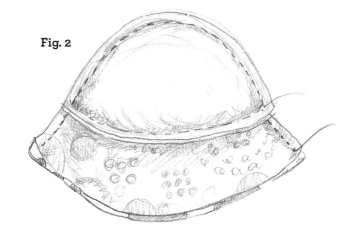

**Fig. 3**

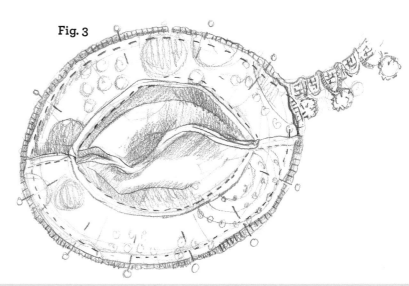

**1** Use the Shell Top template to cut out two pink fleece pieces. Use the Shell Underside pattern to cut out a single orange fleece piece (place straight edge of pattern on the fold). Cut two Shell Rim pieces out of the printed cotton.

**2** Placing right sides together, pin a cotton Shell Rim piece along the edge of each fleece Shell Top. Machine stitch the fabric in place, removing the pins as you stitch (Fig. 1).

Placing right sides together, stack the connected shell pieces. Pin and stitch the two halves of the shell together. Leave the bottom edge unsewn (Fig. 2).

**3** Keeping right sides together, stretch out the shell top so

it covers the orange fleece Shell Underside base. Insert the pom-pom side of the trim between the two layers of fabric, wrapping it around the entire shell edge. Carefully pin it in place so a consistent portion of the trim edge extends outside the fabric (Fig. 3). Allow the pom-pom trim to overlap where the ends meet. Machine stitch around the shell edge, joining the shell to the underside while trapping the trim between the layers. Leave a 2" (5cm) opening at the back of the shell. Turn the shell right side out. Stuff the shell with fiberfill and hand stitch the opening closed, trapping the ends of the trim inside the shell.

**4** Use the Body pattern to cut two body pieces out of the green

fleece (to make one body piece, place the straight edge of the pattern on the fold). Designate one of the Body pieces to be the top Body piece. Cut the notch out of the top Body piece where indicated on the pattern. Use the Head template to cut two piece from green fleece, marking the Neck points on each Head piece.

With right sides together, sew each of the head pieces to the sides of the notch cut out, lining up the straight neck edge with the edges of the notch.

Stack the head pieces right sides together (Fig. 4). Starting from the Neck Point, sew around the top of the head down to the center of the notch. This connects the head to the top of the body.

Stack the Top Body piece and bottom Body piece right sides together. Pin the pieces together.

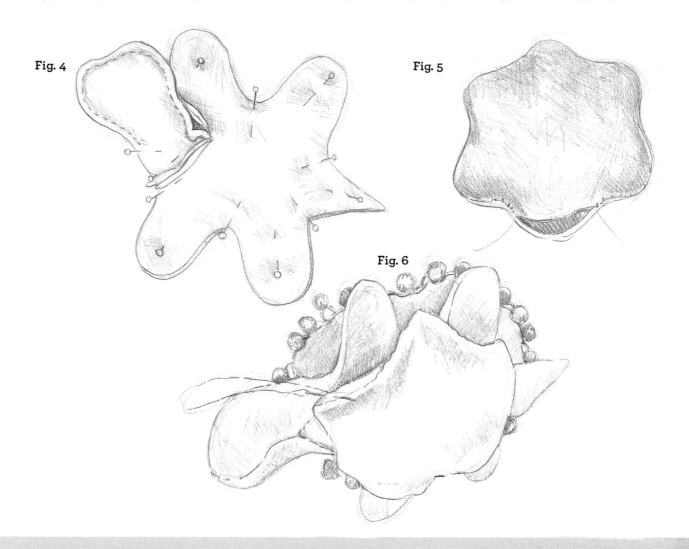

Fig. 4

Fig. 5

Fig. 6

Starting at the Neck Point, sew around either side of the body pieces, stopping just after the back leg. Return to the neck point and sew down the other side of the body, stopping after you've completed stitching the tail. This will leave a gap for you to turn the piece right side out.

Check your seams and turn the body and head right side out. Push stuffing into the head and neck, then fill the four legs and tail. Leave the stomach portion unstuffed. Hand stitch the opening closed.

**5** Cut two Chest pieces, one from yellow fleece and one from dark green felt. Placing right sides together, pin the two pieces together. Stitch around the outside edge and leave an opening. Turn the piece right side out (Fig. 5). Hand stitch the opening closed.

**6** Use the finished chest piece to hold the body against the underside of the shell. Hand stitch each chest point to the underside of the shell, at either side of the neck, at the sides between the two legs and at both sides of the tail. Make multiple small stitches to strengthen the connection and tightly knot the ends (Fig. 6).

**7** Cut and randomly place large felt circles with small felt circles over the top of the turtle shell. Once you're pleased with the arrangement, pin and hand stitch them in place with small invisible stitches. To make the eyes, stitch a black button eye to either side of the head. Draw the thread back and forth across the inside of the head to nestle the buttons against the head. Cut a 1" (2.5cm) white and dark green circle in half. Stack the dark eyelid over the white one and stitch them over the top of each eye.

String the sewing needle with two strands of pink embroidery floss. Hide your knot under one of the button eyes and begin stitching a big smiling mouth with two elongated stitches. Begin at the cheek and end at the neck seam. Repeat the stitch on the other side of the face. Bring the thread across the inside of the head to tighten the stitch and repeat to make a second layer. End by tying a knot under one of the button eyes.

# summer friends

It's hard to resist this adorable trio. Bright and cheery, punctuated with floral cotton prints, they'd make great springtime gifts. All three designs share the same basic construction, pattern pieces and removable wings, but each friend has a unique wing shape and arrangement of felt beads and button embellishments.

## Bug Materials

- ➲ Pattern pieces on pages 123-124
- ➲ ¼ yard 100% wool felt in white for face, arms, legs
- ➲ 6" × 8½" (15cm × 21.5cm) 35% wool felt in green for head, back
- ➲ 4" × 5" (10cm × 12.5cm) 35% wool felt in red for feet
- ➲ 5" × 6" (12.5cm × 15cm) floral printed cotton fabric for belly
- ➲ 9" × 5½" 23cm × 14cm) 100% wool felt in yellow for wings
- ➲ 9" × 5½" (23cm × 14cm) spotted printed fabric for wings
- ➲ Wool scraps in light blue for cheeks
- ➲ Black wool roving
- ➲ Embroidery thread in black
- ➲ Two white felt beads
- ➲ One ½" (1.5cm) red felt bead
- ➲ Two ½" (1.5cm) pink flower buttons
- ➲ Two 11" (28cm) lengths of ¼" (6mm) pink satin ribbon
- ➲ Fiberfill stuffing

## Tools

- ➲ Sewing machine
- ➲ Crewel needle
- ➲ Sewing needle
- ➲ Felting needle
- ➲ Straight pins
- ➲ Scissors
- ➲ Stuffing stick or knitting needle

**Dimensions**

*11" (28cm) high, 9" (23cm) wide, 5" (12.5cm) deep*

# Bug

This is the only kind of bug I'd welcome into my home. Dots and flowers are much more appealing than glossy black beetle wings.

**1**  Cut two Bug Back pieces from green felt. Cut one Bug Forehead piece from the green felt; note the markings from the pattern. Cut one Bug Face piece out of a single layer of white felt. Cut four Bug Leg pieces from the remaining white felt. Cut four Bug Foot pieces out of the red felt. Cut two Bug Wing piece from the spotted fabric and yellow felt (place the straight line indicated on the pattern on the fabric fold). Cut the Bug Belly piece from the floral printed cotton; note the markings from the pattern.

**2**  Pin the Back pieces right sides together, and sew along the seam between the dots indicated on the pattern, leaving the front of the body open. Position the top of the Forehead piece over the Face piece, pin and stitch the bottom edge in place. Pin The arm pieces together to make two arms; stitch them leaving the straight edge open. Pin a Foot piece to the bottom of each Leg piece, matching right sides together, and stitch in place. Next, pin each pair of legs right sides together. Stitch around the outside edge, leaving the straight top open (Fig. 1).

**3**  Place the head piece over the fabric Belly, right sides together. Line up the neck edges and stitch the neck together (Fig. 2).

**4**  Trim away excess fabric and turn the arms and legs right side out. Stuff them with fiberfill, using a knitting needle or stuffing stick to push the fill into the tips of the hands and feet. Pin the arms and legs to the fabric Belly. Machine stitch the top of the arms and legs to the fabric Belly (Fig. 3).

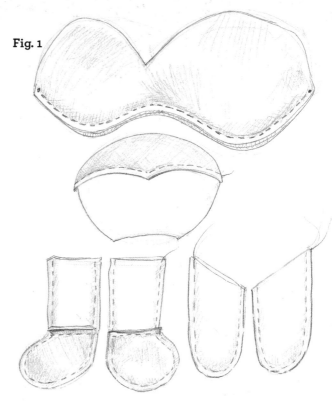

Fig. 1

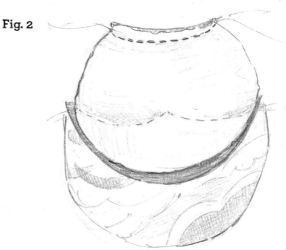

Fig. 2

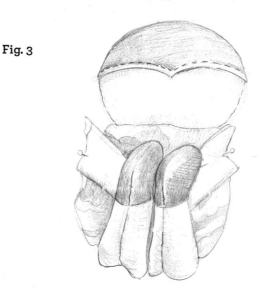

Fig. 3

**5** Position the back piece right side down over the body, trapping the arms and legs inside. Pin the edges together, and stitch all the way around leaving a 2" (5cm) opening beside one of the legs (Fig. 4).

**6** Pull the piece right side out through the opening. Check your seams and then stuff the head and body with fiberfill. Hand stitch the opening closed (Fig. 5).

**7** Pin the fabric and felt wings right sides together. Stitch around the wings, leaving the top open. Trim the fabric edges and turn the wings right side out. Stuff lightly, then pin the ribbon ends inside each edge at the top of the wing. Hand stitch the top closed, trapping the ribbon ends in your stitches.

**8** Finish by adding embellishments. Needle felt small black wool roving eyes directly into either side of the face. With a crewel needle threaded with a full strand of embroidery floss, make two stitches to form a small mouth. Use a sewing needle and white thread to stitch blue felt circle cheeks, a felt bead antennae, a felt nose and a flower button to each shoe. Tie the finished wings around the neck.

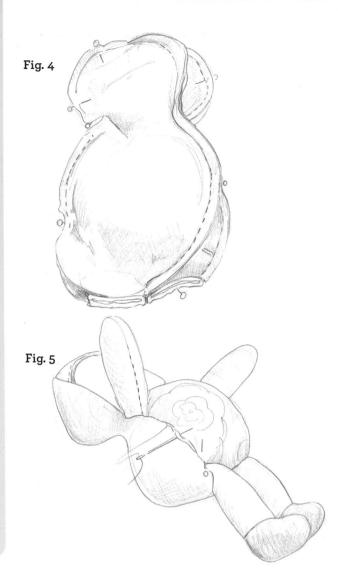

Fig. 4

Fig. 5

# Duck

Unlike your favorite bathtub duck, this feathered friend is soft enough to slip under the covers. You have to get a glimpse of this ducky's upturned back end to fully appreciate its cuteness.

### Duck Instructions

*Made like the bug, the duck substitutes its own body pattern and doesn't have arms. Switch the top head shape to the bonnet template. Use a single orange felt bead for the beak, and needle felt a tuft of yellow roving under the middle of the bonnet. Hand stitch a yellow button to the top of the duck's feet, then stack the flower buttons together and stitch them to the top of the bonnet.*

## Duck Materials

- Pattern pieces on page 124
- 5" × 4" (12.5cm × 10cm) 100% wool felt in white for face
- ¼ yard 100% wool felt in yellow for back, legs
- 5 ½" × 4 ½" (14cm × 11.5cm) floral printed cotton for stomach
- 9 ½ " × 4 ½" (24cm × 11.5cm) 35% felt in pink for wings
- 9 ½" × 4 ½" (24cm × 11.5cm) printed cotton for wings
- 4" × 5" (10cm × 12.5cm) 35% felt in orange for feet
- Black and yellow wool roving
- ½" (1.5cm) orange felt bead
- Two ½" (1.5cm) round buttons
- 1" (2.5cm) felt flower button
- ½" (1.5cm) pink flower button
- Two 11" (28cm) lengths of ¼" (6mm) grosgrain ribbon

### Dimensions

*9" (23cm) high, 11" (28cm) wide, 5 ½" (14cm) deep*

# Bunny

Show some bunny just how much you love them with this furry friend. Not satisfied with just jumping, this rabbit has removable butterfly wings for dress up fun. The trick behind the perky ears is a section of chenille stem.

## Bunny Instructions

*The bunny shares his body pattern with the bug, but he does not have an appliqué at the top of the head. Instead, he needs a pair of ears. Use the template to cut them out of the white wool felt and then pin each pair together. Sew around the outside edges leaving the flat base unsewn. Insert a folded half chenille stem into the opening at the base of the ear. Place the ears point side down on either side of the top of the head. Stitch them in place (your machine should be able to stitch easily over the stem ends). Leave the ears in this downward-facing position*

*while you stitch the back of the body to the front of the body. They should spring up right when you turn the bunny right side out. Hand stitch a felt flower button to the base of one ear, a purple felt bead nose to the middle of the face, and a green felt bead to each foot. Cluster the*

*three felt flowers together to make a tail, and stitch them to his bottom. Embroider whiskers on either side of the face. Finish by making a small smiling mouth.*

## Bunny Materials

- Pattern pieces on pages 123-124
- ¼ yard 100% wool felt in white for face, legs, arms, ears
- 6" × 8 ½" (15cm × 21.5cm) 35% wool felt in pink for back
- 8" × 8" (20.5cm × 20.5cm) spotted printed cotton for wings
- 8" × 8" (20.5cm × 20.5cm) 35% wool felt in red for wings
- 5" × 6" (12.5cm × 15cm) printed cotton for the belly
- 4" × 5" (10cm × 12.5cm) 100% wool felt in yellow for feet
- One purple felt bead
- Two green ½" (1.5cm) felt beads
- Fiberfill stuffing
- Two 11" (28cm) lengths of ¼" (6mm) pink grosgrain ribbon
- Chenille stems (cut in half with wire cutters)
- Pink and black embroidery floss
- 1" (2.5cm) pink felt flower button
- Three small yellow felt flowers

### Dimensions

11" (28cm) high, 8" (20.5cm) wide, 5 ½" (14cm) deep

# hilarious hoots

It's hard not to smile when you look at these owls. Their bright colors and fanciful eyes make them appeal to young and old alike. This pattern was intentionally designed to require very little hand stitching. The pairing of felt and fleece on the wings and feet gives them stability and structure without traditional interfacing. A die cut machine is a must to cut out the wonderful flower- and circle-shaped eyes.

## Materials

- ⟳ Pattern pieces on page 124
- ⟳ 18" × 7" (45.5cm × 18cm) piece of printed cotton for chest
- ⟳ 6" × 8" (15cm × 20.5cm) coordinating piece of printed cotton for back of head
- ⟳ ¼ yard of fleece for top of head, lower back
- ⟳ ¼ yard of fleece for wings for feet
- ⟳ ¼ yard of felt for wings for feet
- ⟳ Two 1" (2.5cm) colored buttons
- ⟳ Two ⅓" (1cm) black buttons
- ⟳ Thread
- ⟳ Fiberfill
- ⟳ Additional scraps of colored felt to make flowers and circles for eyes, beak

## Tools

- ⟳ Sewing machine
- ⟳ Sewing needle
- ⟳ Straight pins
- ⟳ Scissors
- ⟳ Die cut machine with flower and circle templates
- ⟳ Stuffing stick or knitting needle

**Dimensions**
*8" (20.5cm) high, 9" (23cm) wide, 9" (23cm) deep*

**1** Cut four Wing pieces, two from felt and two from fleece. Cut two Feet pieces, one from fleece and one from felt. Fold the printed cotton in half and cut two Chest pieces. Fold the fleece in half and cut two Lower Back pieces. Cut the Top of Head pattern from the fleece and the Back of Head piece from coordinating cotton fabric.

**2** Pair the felt and fleece wing pieces together, right sides out. Pin and then machine stitch around the outside edge, creating a decorative loop starting between the wing feathers. Arc your seam into the middle of the wing. With the sewing needle in place, lift the presser foot and swivel the fabric to create the point in the middle of the loop. Arc your seam back down the edge of the wing. Leave the straight edge of the wing unsewn. Repeat the process with the second wing.

Pair the felt foot with the fleece foot, right sides out. Pin and stitch them together making a continuous seam around the entire outside edge. Slow down to go around each of the toes.

Pin the chest pieces, right sides together, and seam the inside edge together in one straight seam. Pin the lower back pieces together then stitch down the inside back and to the marking halfway across the base. This corner will form the tail (Fig. 1). Trim the felt fabric on the toes to contour the fleece toes.

**3** Working on the back of the owl, trap the flat section of the wings between the lower back and cotton (back of the head) headpiece. Pin and then stitch through all the layers to anchor the wings in place (Fig. 2).

**Fig. 1**

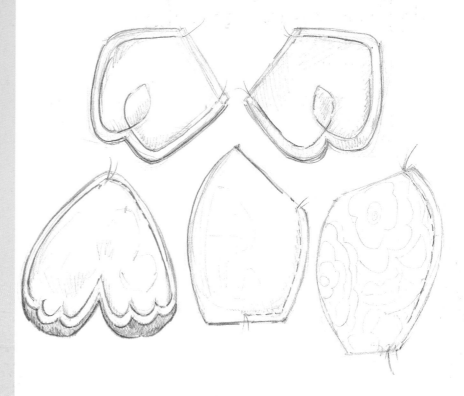

**Fig. 2**

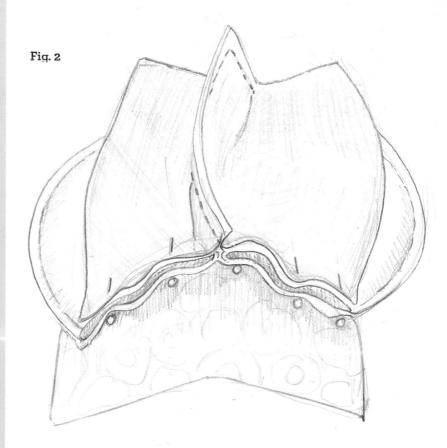

**4** Working on the front of the owl, pin the bottom edge of the fleece (front) headpiece to the top edge of the chest piece. Machine stitch them together (Fig. 3).

**5** To prepare the back of the owl for stitching, fold up and pin the wings so they won't get caught in the side seams (Fig. 4).

**6** Pin the front and back pieces right sides together, being careful to line up the head seams. Make a continuous seam around the owl, leaving the base unsewn. Trim the corners. Pull the piece right side out, being mindful of the straight

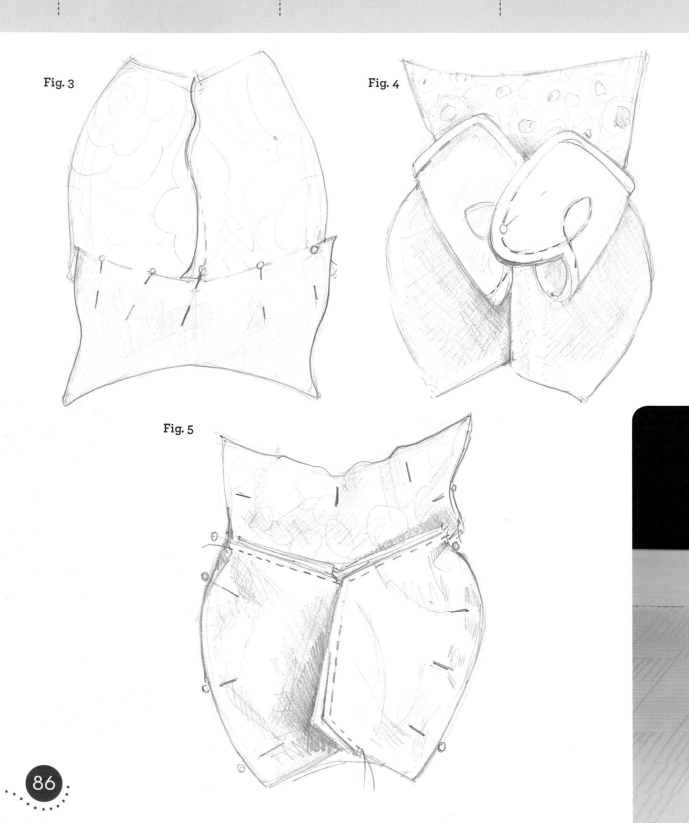

Fig. 3

Fig. 4

Fig. 5

pin trapped inside. Check your seams, especially around the wings (Fig. 5).

**7** Use a stuffing stick or knitting needle to fill the ears and then tightly stuff the rest of the body. Hand stitch the opening closed. Position the foot over the sewn base so the toes emerge under the belly. Pin and hand stitch it in place (Fig. 6).

**8** To make the beak, fold a felt circle in half. Whipstitch the edge together, stopping halfway to fill it with stuffing. Stitch it to the center base of the head. Next, hand stitch stacked flowers and buttons in place for the eyes. To make sleepy eyes, cut a felt circle in half and hand stitch the tops of the half circles in place.

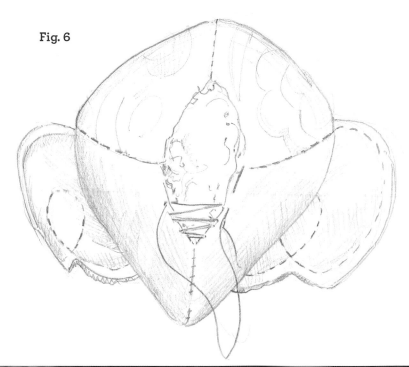

Fig. 6

## ChapterFour

# felt and fabric

Irresistible to touch, the whimsical projects in this chapter feature unique felt and fabric pairings. A simple design becomes something extraordinary by juxtaposing different fabric colors, patterns, weights and textures. Sometimes switching just one of the fabrics will make all the difference. I wasn't satisfied with the *Mushroom Pincushion* design on page 94 until I decided to change the plain felt stem to corduroy; the unexpected textural addition made the project more interesting.

The *Little Hoots and Lelephants* (page 102) showcase patterned fabric on their bellies and recycled wool felt wings. Thinner felt backs, feet and layered flower eyes add more color and another fabric weight; the same vibrant pairings make up the engaging Lelephant. The *Tweet Needle Case* (page 106) features felt that makes a clean background for the fabric bird appliqué. Roles are reversed on the inside where pattern fabric creates the background for the felt needle strips and flower embellishments.

The colors of the *Felt and Flannel Trio* (page 90) are more subdued, but the combination of fabric textures is still key. The soft patterned flannel and the natural antibacterial properties of wool make them ideal fabric for children's playthings. The happy little *Birds in a Nest* (page 98) feature multiple layers of different felt colors and varieties. Pinking shears and decorative stitching in the wings add texture, depth and detail to the simple design, and the addition of patterned fabric in the nest lining provides interest and whimsy.

Whether you prefer the punch of bright colors or the quiet beauty of soft colors, experiment with the texture in your stash and enjoy the results.

# felt and flannel trio

Soft to the touch, flannel and felt are a fabulous tactile pairing for children's softies. The sturdy knotted flannel tails are perfect for little hands to grab and carry. The size, shape and scale of these three designs are varied at first glance, but it might surprise you to discover that they're constructed the same way. An underbelly piece fits in between the two sides, and the folded ear pieces are sewn into slits.

## Giraffe Materials

- ➲ Pattern pieces on page 125
- ➲ 24" × 7 ½" (61cm x 19cm) 100% wool felt in orange for body
- ➲ 5" (12.5cm) square of light green 35% wool felt for underside, ears
- ➲ Scraps of bamboo felt in brown for spots
- ➲ 12" × 16 ½" (30.5cm × 42cm) piece of printed flannel for tail, ossicones, ears
- ➲ Embroidery floss in brown, ochre
- ➲ Sewing thread in off-white
- ➲ Fiberfill stuffing

## Tools

- ➲ Sewing machine
- ➲ Straight pins
- ➲ Scissors
- ➲ Sewing needle
- ➲ Crewel needle
- ➲ Stuffing stick or knitting needle
- ➲ Die cut machine with ¾" (2cm), 1" (2.5cm) and 1 ½" (4cm) circle templates

**Dimensions**
10 ½" × 6 ½" (26.5cm × 16.5cm)

# Giraffe

This enduring giraffe features spotted flannel and whimsical spots.

**1** Cut four Giraffe Ear pieces, two from out of both the printed flannel and the light green felt. Cut a 3 1/2" x 5" (9cm x 12.5cm) strip of flannel for the tail and two 2 1/2" x 5" (6.5cm x 12.5cm) strips for the ossicones. Pin each pair of felt and flannel ears, right sides together (Fig. 1), then stitch around the outside edge, leaving the flat bottom edge unsewn (Fig. 2). Fold and pin each of the three strips in half, right sides together (Fig. 1). Stitch the open top and sides together, leaving the bottom unsewn.

**2** Trim away any excess fabric, especially from the corners of the ears and strips. Turn the pieces right side out. It may be helpful to use a knitting needle or stuffing stick to reach all the way into the thin strips. Make a second topstitch seam around the outside edge of the ears, leaving the bottom edge unsewn. Tie an overhand knot in each of the strips 1 1/4" (3cm) from the end of the tail, 3/4" (2cm) from the end of the ossicones (Fig. 2).

**3** Cut two Giraffe Body pieces from the orange felt. As indicated on the template, cut two slits in each head area of the body pieces. Cut the Giraffe Underside piece from the light green felt. Working on the wrong side of the head, insert the small knotted ossicone, open end first, through the first slit, and pin in place. Fold the ear along the line indicated on the template. Insert and pin it into the second opening. Turn the piece right side up to check the placement of both pieces. Make sure you're happy with the length of the knotted strip and that the flannel portion of the ear will be facing out. Repeat the pinning process to add the remaining ear and small knotted ossicone to the other side of the head. Make individual straight seams to trap each of the pinned pieces in place (Fig. 3). Check your seams and then trim away any excess fabric.

**Fig. 1**

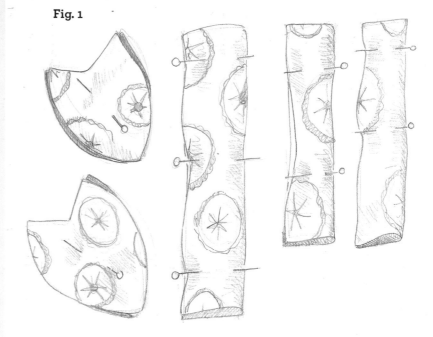

**Fig. 2**

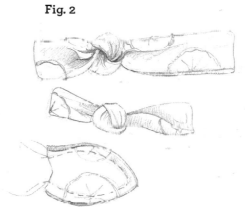

**TIP**

The small "antennae" on the top of a giraffe's head are called ossicones.

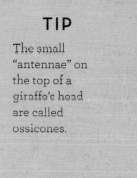

**Fig. 3**

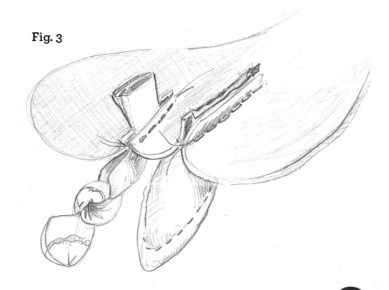

**4** Stack the two body pieces right sides together, then pin the back and head together. Be careful to line up the seams in the head. Insert the Underside piece between the sides. Pin the legs, neck and bottom in place. Insert the long knotted tail strip into the giraffe's bottom; position it just above the end of the bottom piece so it's trapped between the two orange sides (Fig. 4). Machine stitch around the entire giraffe, leaving a 3" (7.5cm) opening at the back of the hind leg. Check all your seams and flip the animal over to make sure you grabbed all the fabric edges.

**5** Carefully pull the piece right side out. Start by pushing the head down towards the neck and out through the opening. A stuffing stick or knitting needle will help in this process. Pull the rest of the giraffe right side out through the opening. Begin stuffing by pushing fiberfill up into the nose; continue stuffing it full—you don't want a wobbly neck. Hand stitch the opening closed (Fig. 5).

**6** Cut the spots from the brown felt. Use a sewing needle to sew three brown circles to each side of the giraffe's body. Switch to a crewel needle and a full strand of ochre floss to embroider an enlarged double cross-stitch on the center of each of the circles (Fig. 6). Switch to a full strand of brown floss to make French-knotted eyes and a small stitched mouth.

Fig. 4

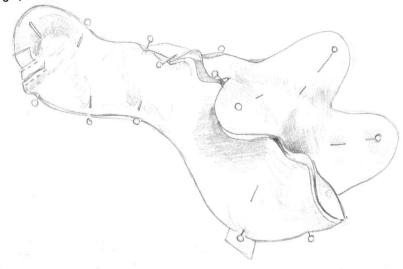

Fig. 6

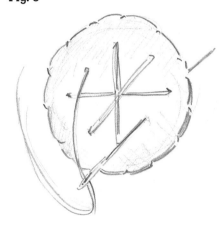

Fig. 5

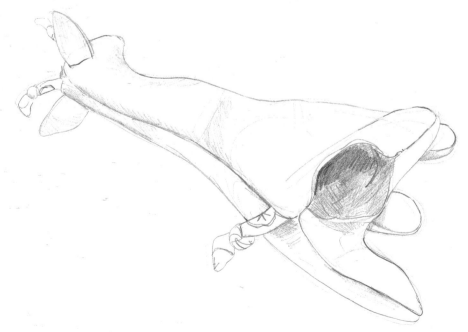

# Elephant

I love the swoop of this elephant's trunk and his floppy ears. The plain felt background will perfectly frame the patterned flannel you select for the ears. Embroidered eyes and no loose pieces make this an ideal choice for a toddler.

### Elephant Instructions

*Follow the directions for the giraffe, substituting the elephant templates and using a 2 1/2" × 6" (6.5cm × 15cm) strip for the tail. Skip the directions for the spots and the knotted ossicones.*

## Materials

- Pattern pieces on page 125
- 12" × 16" (30.5cm × 40.5cm) piece of 35% wool felt in light blue for the body
- 18 1/2" × 19" (47cm × 48.5cm) piece of 35% wool felt in dark blue for the underbelly, ears
- 8" × 12" (20.5cm × 30.5cm) striped flannel for ears, tail
- Embroidery thread in light and dark blue
- Sewing thread
- Fiberfill stuffing

## Tools (for remaining creatures)

- Sewing machine
- Sewing needle
- Crewel needle
- Straight pins
- Scissors

### Dimensions

10" × 6" (25.5cm × 15cm)

# Mouse

My mother always stashed a little mouse in my dad's briefcase for luck. This pocket-sized fellow has so much character he's sure to spread smiles.

### Mouse Instructions

*The mouse is made like the other animals except for the additions of the felt bead nose and embroidered straight-stitched whiskers, and using a 2" × 5 1/2" (5cm × 14cm) strip for the tail. If you're making him/her for a very small child, skip the bead nose, which presents a choking hazard if it's pulled off.*

## Materials

- Pattern pieces on page 125
- 8" × 6" (20.5cm × 15cm) piece of 35% wool felt in dark pink for body
- 5" × 6" (12.5cm × 15cm) piece of 35% wool felt in light pink for underside, ears
- 6" × 11 1/2" (15cm × 29cm) printed flannel for ears, tail
- Embroidery floss in brown, white
- 1/3" (1cm) felt bead

### Dimensions

5" × 3" (12.5cm × 7.5cm) plus a 4" (10cm) tail

# mushroom pincushion

The epitome of whimsy, these mushrooms are guaranteed to put a smile on your face. Use them in your sewing room to collect pins or assemble a decorative grouping to display in your living space. They're a beautiful accompaniment to the deer and gnomes. Brightly colored felt is paired with printed fabric and corduroy for a blending of textures and colors. The spots are appliquéd to the top of the mushroom with a circle of blanket stitch. The corduroy stems are filled with paper pet bedding to give the finished mushrooms stability.

I've stepped out the red mushroom with white spots but have included instructions to make the variations. Have fun creating your own signature mushroom by varying the length of the corduroy stem and changing the fabric, felt and floss colors.

## Materials

### Red Mushroom

- ➲ Pattern pieces on page 125
- ➲ 7 1/4" × 3 3/4" (18.5cm x 9.5cm) rectangle of wide wale white corduroy
- ➲ Scrap of printed cotton
- ➲ 35% wool felt in red, white, mustard, green
- ➲ Embroidery floss in green
- ➲ Sewing thread
- ➲ Paper pet bedding
- ➲ Fiberfill stuffing

### Orange Mushroom

- ➲ Use all the same materials and tools listed above but omit the printed cotton and switch the following items to:
- ➲ 2 3/4" × 6" (7cm x 15cm) narrow white corduroy for stem
- ➲ 35% wool felt in dark and light orange, dark brown, beige
- ➲ Embroidery floss in brown

### Flat Mushroom

- ➲ Use all the same materials and tools listed above but switch the follow items to:
- ➲ 2 3/4" × 5 1/2" (7cm x 14cm) piece of beige corduroy for the flat top mushroom
- ➲ 35% wool felt in green, dark brown, mustard
- ➲ Embroidery floss in beige

## Tools

- ➲ Sewing machine
- ➲ Crewel and sewing needles
- ➲ Die cut machine with 3/4" (2cm) and 1 1/4" (3cm) circle templates
- ➲ Hot glue and melt sticks

### Dimensions

*Red Mushroom: 7 1/2" ( 19cm) high x 4 1/2" (11.5cm) wide at cap plus 2 1/2" (6.5cm) stem*

*Orange Mushroom: 6" ( 15cm) high x 4" (10cm) wide at cap plus 2 1/2" (6.5cm) stem*

*Flat Mushroom: 4 1/2" (11.5cm) high x 5" (12.5cm) wide at cap plus 2 1/2" (6.5cm) stem*

**1** Cut two Red Top pieces from the red felt. Cut one Red Underside from the printed cotton. (For the flat top mushroom, cut a top piece from the patterned fabric, and the bottom piece from the green felt from the same Underside pattern).

Cut a 5 ¼" (13.5cm) diameter circle from mustard felt. Fold the felt circle in half and cut four irregular darts from the outside edge into the center. When you unfold the felt you'll have formed the mushroom gills. (You can cut darts and leave the outer edge intact, like the orange mushroom, or cut away the edge like the other mushrooms.)

**2** Place the felt gills over the center of the right side of the fabric Underside. Thread the sewing machine with contrasting bright thread. Working out from the center, stitch up and down each spoke of the gills (Fig. 1). Placing right sides together, pin and stitch the Red Top pieces together, leaving the bottom edge unstitched.

**3** With right sides together, stretch the connected Top over the Underside, and pin the edges together. Stitch around the outside edge, leaving a 1" (2.5cm) opening to turn the mushroom cap right side out (Fig. 2).

**4** Cut a 2" (5cm) diameter circle out of green felt. Cut a 1 ¼" × 7 ¼" (3cm × 18.5cm) felt strip and lay it over the top edge of the corduroy stem. Machine stitch the top edge of the felt collar to the corduroy (Fig. 3). Placing right sides together, align the bottom edge of the corduroy with the edge of the felt circle. Slowly work your way around the circle, moving the corduroy in position over the felt

Fig. 1

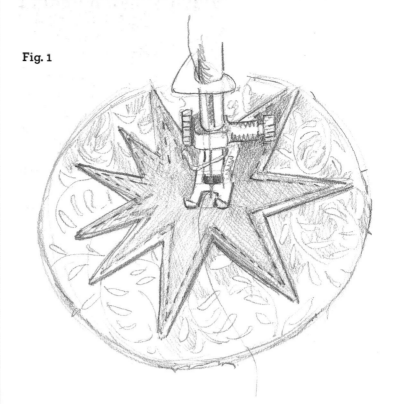

Fig. 2

Fig. 3

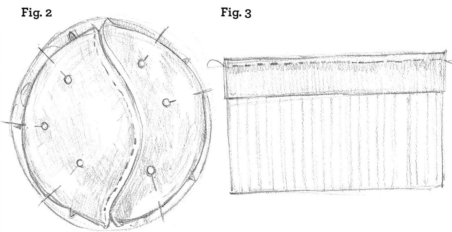

Fig. 4

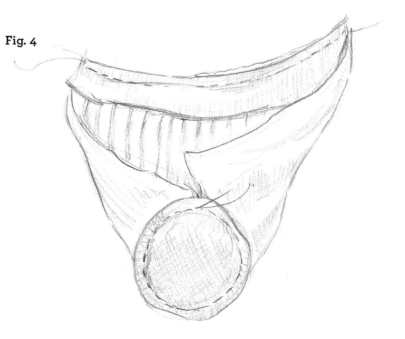

**Fig. 5**

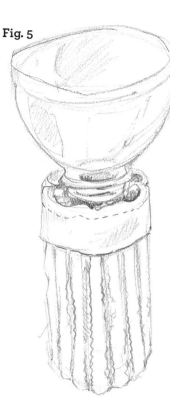

**TIP**

Cut the top off a plastic water bottle to make a funnel to slide the pet bedding into (fig. 5). This will cut down on mess and prevent the bedding from sticking to the felt and corduroy.

**Fig. 6**

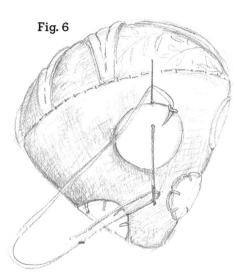

# Flower-Topped Straight Pins

Poke your mushroom with a sprinkling of small felt flower pins. They're reminiscent of the tiny buds on the forest floor.

### Flower-Topped Straight Pin Instructions

*Slide a flower just under the plastic bead at the top of the pin. Squeeze a tiny drop of hot glue under the bead then push the flower up into the glue. Repeat the process to make a few decorative pins for each mushroom.*

## Materials

- ➲ Straight pins
- ➲ Felt scrapbooking flowers

## Tools

- ➲ Hot glue and melt sticks

edge (Fig. 4). After encircling the base, end the seam and cut the thread. Fold the stem flat, bringing the cut edges of the sides together. Make a slightly diagonal seam that starts at the top of the stem and flares out at the base. Turn the stem right side out.

**5** Stuff the mushroom cap with fiberfill and the base with the paper pet bedding (Fig. 5, see Tip at left). Firmly pack the base to give your mushroom stability.

**6** Use the die cut machine to cut circles from the white felt (cut brown spots for the flat top mushroom and green spots for the orange top mushroom). Thread the crewel needle with three strands of green embroidery floss. Insert the needle through the opening and out through the edge of a spot. Begin making a blanket stitch around the outside edge of the spot. To do this pierce the needle 1/4" (6mm) from the outside edge of the spot (Fig. 6).

Continue working your way around the spot, hooking the last stitch to the first before passing the needle through the inside of the cap to the next spot. After all the spots have been encircled in stitches, knot the end. Switch to a sewing needle and thread, and hand stitch the opening closed.

**7** Hand stitch the top of the stem to the underside of the mushroom. Encircle the connection at least twice, lifting the felt collar up to check your connection. Snip the collar at 1/4" (6mm) intervals to create a decorative fringe.

# birds in a nest

Feather your nest with these charming layered-felt birds. Bluebirds are a symbol of happiness, so I chose to sew the design in a selection of blue and pink felts. You could easily switch the colors to red and orange for cardinals, or yellow and black to make orioles. These cheery birds fit perfectly in the palm of your hand, and they're irresistible to children.

## Materials

**Female bird**
- ↪ ⅛ yard of 35% wool felt in light pink, light blue
- ↪ ⅛ yard of XoticFelt in aqua

**Male bird**
- ↪ ⅛ yard 35% wool felt in light blue, aqua, teal
- ↪ ⅛ yard of XoticFelt in aqua

**Both Birds**
- ↪ Pattern pieces on page 126
- ↪ Stiffened pink felt
- ↪ Four 6mm black safety eyes
- ↪ Thread
- ↪ Fiberfill stuffing

## Tools

- ↪ Sewing machine
- ↪ Sewing needle
- ↪ Straight pins
- ↪ Scissors
- ↪ Pinking shears
- ↪ Hot glue gun and melt sticks

**Dimensions**
6" × 4" (15cm × 10cm)

**Fig. 1**

**Fig. 2**

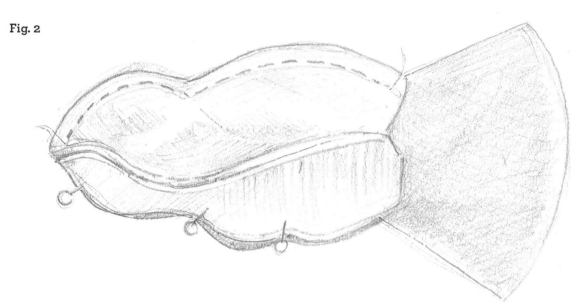

**1** Cut the Bird Base, Top, Side, Wing Base and Wing Top pieces out of felt. Select the lightest shade for the Base piece and Wing Base. (Note: for the Wing Base, use the Wing Base/Middle pattern; cut the bottom portion of the piece slightly longer than the pattern, but keep the rounded top and edges the same size.) Use a medium shade for the Side and Wing Middle. The darkest shade is for the Top and Wing Top.

Position one of the Side body pieces along one edge of the Top body piece. Machine stitch the edges together (Fig. 1).

**2** Position the remaining Side along the other edge of the Top piece. Pin it in place and then make a second seam to connect it to the outside edge (Fig. 2).

**3** Separate the Side pieces and position the Base body piece between them. Make a continuous seam around the outside edge connecting the Base piece to the Side pieces and tail. Leave a small opening where indicated on the pattern. Flatten the sides and stitch together the head portion of the Side pieces where they meet between the Top of the head and the chest portion of the Base (Fig. 3). Turn the body right side out. Flatten the tail and topstitch a decorative elongated zigzag pattern with three points (refer to the stitch lines on the pattern piece for placement).

**4** Stack Wing Middle pieces over the Wing Base pieces. Align your presser foot with the outside edge of the wings and topstitch to connect the pieces and make a decorative detail (refer to the pattern, see Turning a Corner on page 15).

Use pinking shears to trim the bottom edge of the Wing Top pieces, then place them over the wing portion you just stitched. Topstitch a half circle seam around the edge of the Wing Top (Fig. 4).

**5** Use scissor points to clip a small opening cut on either side of the head approximately ½" (1.5cm) from the seam down the center of the face and insert one of the safety eyes (see Adding Safety Eyes on page 16). Repeat the process to insert and stabilize the second eye. Tightly stuff the bird with fiberfill and hand stitch the opening closed. Position the wings on either side of the body. Hand stitch the top section of the wing to the body. Hide your stitches around the top section in the first layer of felt. Cut the Beak out of stiffened felt and hot glue it to the bird face.

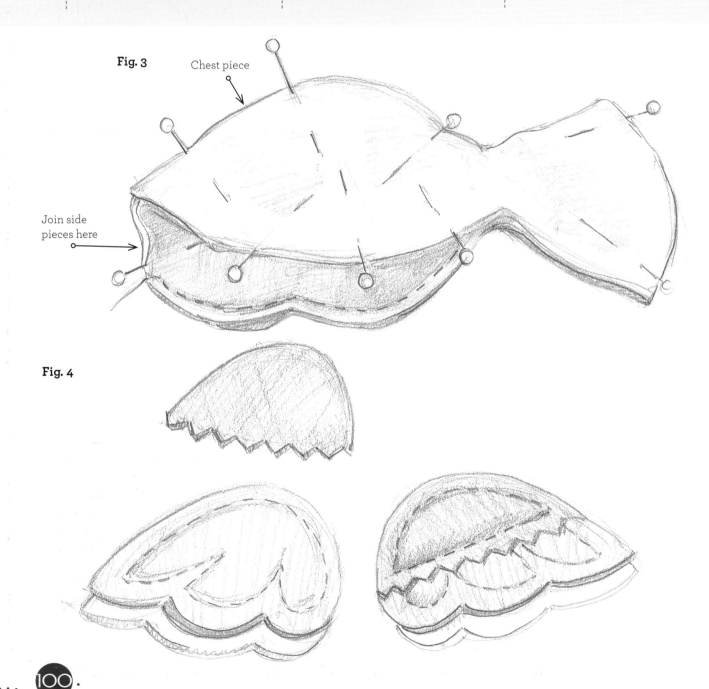

**Fig. 3**

Chest piece

Join side pieces here

**Fig. 4**

# Nest

Give your happy friends a place to rest!

**Fig. 5**

**Fig. 6**

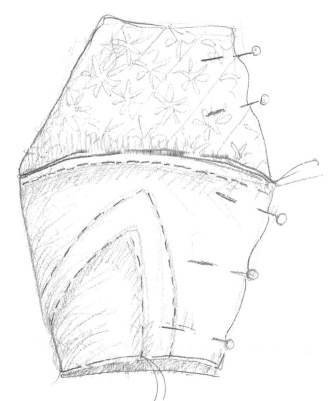

## Materials

➔ Pattern pieces on page 126
➔ ¼ yard 100% wool felt in putty
➔ Scrap of 100% wool felt in white
➔ Scraps of 35% wool felt in light blue, pink
➔ Scrap of XoticFelt in aqua
➔ Printed cotton

## Tools

➔ Sewing machine
➔ Sewing needle
➔ Straight pins
➔ Scissors

## Dimensions

2 ½" (6.5cm) tall with an approximately 4" × 3" (10cm × 7.5cm) opening

**1** Cut the Nest Base piece out of both cotton and felt. Cut Leaf Sets 1 and 2 out of colored felt. Stack the smaller leaf shapes over the larger ones and pin them to the felt nest piece, lining the straight leaf edges with the bottom of the Nest Base. Topstitch the leaf shapes in place, aligning your presser foot along the outside edges of the shapes (see Turning a Corner on page 15). (Fig. 5).

**2** Stack the felt Nest Base piece over the cotton Nest Base piece, placing right sides together. Pin them and sew a single seam along the top edge. Separate the layers and refold the connected fabric in half lengthwise. Be sure to keep the right sides on the inside, and pin the cut edges together. Starting with the cotton fabric, make a continuous straight seam down through the felt and across the open felt edge. Turn the piece right sides out. Bring together the open edges of the cotton liner. Tuck in ¼" (6mm) of the fabric edge, pin (Fig. 6), and machine stitch closed. Push the liner down into the finished nest.

Fold down the top edge the nest to show off the fabric lining.

# little hoots and lelephants

Irresistible pocket-sized softies can be loved as toys, hung as ornaments or assembled as a grouping to make a captivating mobile. Heavyweight felted sweater fabric gives stability to the elephant ears and owl's wings. Lighter felt is used for the elephant's tail and inner ears, and the owl's beak, feet and fabric eyes. The biggest burst of color comes from the patterned cotton fabric. Have fun playing with different color combinations.

A note of caution: If you're making these softies as play-things for young children, skip the button eyes and hanging strings that could become choking/safety hazards.

## Little Hoots Materials

- Pattern pieces on page 126
- Printed cotton for chest
- 35% wool felt scraps in assorted colors for the body, feet, flowers, circles
- 6" square of printed fabric
- Felted sweater fabric for wings
- Two $5/8$" (1.5cm) button eyes
- Two $3/8$" (1cm) button eyes
- Embroidery floss
- $1 1/2$" (4cm) length of $1/4$" (6mm) wide ribbon
- Sewing thread
- Fiberfill stuffing

## Tools

- Sewing machine
- Sewing needle
- Straight pins
- Scissors
- Die cut machine with $1 3/4$" (4.5cm) flower and 1" (2.5cm) circle templates
- Hot glue gun and melt sticks
- Stuffing stick or knitting needle

**Dimensions**
*$4 1/2$" (11.5cm) high, $7 1/2$" (19cm) wide at wings, 2" (5cm) deep*

## Little Hoots

I've frantically stitched these owls for the last two holiday fair seasons. They're crowd-pleasers that literally fly out the door. The biggest challenge is keeping them in stock. Choose your own combinations of felt, fabric, flowers and button eyes to give each owl a unique personality.

### TIP

If you don't have a die cut machine, you can substitute felt buttons or hand-cut $1 3/4$" (4.5cm) felt flowers and 1" (2.5cm) circles to complete the eyes.

**1** Cut two Body pieces, one out from printed cotton and one from felt. Cut one Feet piece out of the felt (do not add a seam allowance to the foot piece). Cut two Wing pieces out of felted sweater fabric.

**2** Lay the felt Body on your work surface. Stack the Wings over the center of the Body. The wing tips should face toward the inside and the connection should extend ¼" (6mm) beyond the Body piece. Place the Feet, curved edge up, over the bottom of the Body piece. The ends of the feet should extend below the bottom of the body (Fig. 1). Lay the cotton Body piece right side down, aligning it with the felt body piece and trapping the wings and felt pieces between the layers. Fold the ribbon in half and slip it, fold side down, between the body layers at the top of the head.

**3** Pin the edges together and make a seam around the outside edge of the body, leaving a 1" (2.5cm) opening to one side of the head. Check that you caught both the wings, feet and ribbon hanger in your seam. Trim away the excess fabric and turn the body right side out. Stuff the body and hand stitch the opening closed.

**4** Cut two felt flowers and two circles with your die cut machine.

**5** Stack the flowers, circles and buttons together to make elaborate eyes. Hand stitch them in place with a sewing needle and thread, and hide your knots under the felt pieces. Thread your crewel needle with a full strand of floss and make decorative straight stitches around the felt flowers and circles. String the remaining floss through the ribbon loop, and tie the ends in an overhand knot to make a hanging loop.

Snip a small triangular felt beak from the desired felt and hot glue it between the eyes.

**Fig. 1**

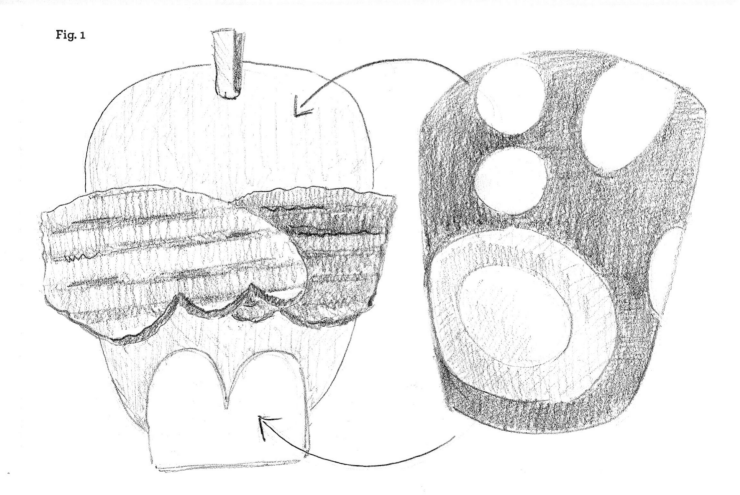

# Lelephant

Simple to stitch together, these elephants have big personality. The key is to select coordinating patterned fabrics for the head and body. Next, find complementary felt for the ears and tail.

**Fig. 2**

## Materials

- Pattern pieces on page 126
- Two printed cotton fabrics; 8" square for head, 12" square for body
- Two colors of 35% wool felt scraps for ears
- 1/2" × 3 1/2" (1.5cm × 9cm) strip of 35% wool for tail
- Two 3/8" (1cm) button eyes
- Two 5/8" (1.5cm) button eyes
- Embroidery floss
- 1 1/2" (4cm) piece of 1/4" (6mm) wide ribbon
- Sewing thread
- Fiberfill stuffing

## Tools

- Sewing machine
- Sewing needle
- Straight pins
- Scissors
- Stuffing stick or knitting needle

### Dimensions

4 1/2" (11.5cm) high, 5 1/4" (13.5cm) wide, 6" (15cm) wide ear span, 2 1/2" (6.5cm) deep

**1** Cut two Outer Ears and two Inner Ears from the different colored felts. Place an Inner Ear inside each Outer Ear. Set your machine on the zigzag setting and stitch around the outside of the Inner Ear. Your stitches should span from the inside ear to the outside ear so the pieces are sewn together. For the tail, tie the end of the wool strip into an overhand knot.

**2** Cut two Head and Body pieces out of the printed fabrics. Lay the body pieces right side up on your work surface (Fig. 2). Place an ear faceup in the center of the diagonal neckline. Lay the Head piece right side down over the ear, and pin the diagonal edges together. Machine stitch a seam down the diagonal neck edge, joining the Head to the Body and anchoring the ear in between.

**3** Pin the ear flaps down to the body to keep them out of the way for the next seam. Placing right sides together, stack one body piece over the other. Pin the legs, trunk, head and back together. Fold the ribbon and insert it, folded end down, between the fabric layers at the beginning of the back. Pin it in place. Insert the tail knot, end first, between the elephant's behind, and pin it in place. Machine stitch a seam around the outside edge of the elephant, leaving an opening under the tail.

**4** Trim the fabric and turn the piece right side out. Use a stuffing stick or knitting needle to push stuffing down into the trunk and the legs, and then stuff the rest of the body. Hand stitch the opening closed. Stack the smaller buttons over the larger beads and stitch them to the sides of the head. Thread the crewel needle with a full strand of embroidery floss and blanket stitch around the outside of each ear (see Blanket Stitch on page 17). Switch floss colors and thread a hanging string from the ribbon loop. Finish by tying the ends in an overhand knot.

# tweet needle case

One of the first steps in becoming a sewer is to equip your self as one. Losing track of your sewing needles can be a dangerous event. This handy case has a protective cardboard lining and two rows of felt to pierce your needles into. The clever bird-leg closure is simply an elastic loop that hooks over a handmade fabric-covered button. Whether you slip it in your sewing bag or take pride in displaying it on your coffee table, you'll always know where your needles are.

## Materials

- 8 1/2" × 3 3/4" (21.5cm × 9.5cm) bright pink 35% felt for the front
- 8 1/2" × 3 3/4" (21.5cm × 9.5cm) printed cotton fabric for the inside plus scraps for the bird, button
- Two pieces of 1 3/4" × 3" (4.5cm × 7.5cm) yellow felt for the needle strip plus scraps for the beak, wing
- Two pieces of 1 1/8" × 3" (3cm × 7.5cm) light purple 100% wool felt for the needle strip
- 5 1/2" (14cm) black elastic cord
- 1" (2.5cm) metal button cover
- Scrap of fusible interfacing
- Pink thread
- One 8" × 3" (20.5cm × 7.5cm) rectangle of cereal box cardboard
- Two black E beads
- Felt flowers

## Tools

- Sewing machine
- Sewing needle
- Straight pins
- Scissors
- Pinking shears
- Iron
- Stuffing stick or knitting needle

**Dimensions**
3 1/4" × 8" (8.5cm × 20.5cm)

**Fig. 1**

**Fig. 2**

### TIP

There are two different varieties of button covers on the market. One uses a simple cup and lid, the second has teeth. Either variety will work fine.

**1** Lay out the felt front and patterned cotton inside pieces. Cut the two yellow inside needle strips with regular scissors, and then use pinking shears to cut the two smaller light purple strips. Follow the package enclosed instructions to iron fusible interfacing to the underside of the cotton scrap. Use cut a simple bird shape out of the backed cotton. Next, cut the wing and beak shapes from the felt scraps (Fig. 1).

**2** Place the front and back pieces right side up on your work surface. Stack the smaller felt strips over the larger ones. Pin them to the cotton, positioning one pair ¾" (2cm) from the top, and the second 1 ¾" (4.5cm) up from the bottom. The pieces are offset, so when the finished case is folded in half, the rows of needles will stack over each other. Remove the paper backing from the bird and iron it to the felt front, 1 ¼" (3cm) from the base. For the closure, tie each end of the elastic cord in an overhand knot (Fig. 2).

**3** Set your sewing machine to a medium (3) zigzag stitch with the smallest stitch length (0 1). Starting on the center back of the bird, position the needle at the fabric edge. The stitch should stretch between the felt and fabric, straddling the cut edge. Stop on your way down from the bird's head, lift the presser foot and insert the beak. Continue to stitch so the edge of the beak becomes trapped in your stitches. Return the machine to a straight stitch and medium stitch length to sew the felt wing over the fabric bird.

Follow the package instructions to cover the button in coordinating fabric and then hand stitch it over the base of the wing (Fig. 3). Hand stitch an E bead eye to the bird's head. Make two straight seams to connect each pair of needle strips to the cotton.

**4** Stack the front and back pieces right sides together and insert the elastic between the two layers. The knots should extend beyond the fabric edges. Trap the elastic in the pins so the ends stay ³/₄" (2cm) apart. Continue pinning the fabric layers together

at the corners and sides (Fig. 4). Begin stitching at one corner and work up one side and across the top. When you pass over each elastic, reverse and stitch across it again to strengthen the seam. Continue stitching down the other side. Leave the bottom edge unstitched.

**5** Trim the extra fabric from the corners and turn the needle case right side out. Use a knitting needle or stuffing stick to help push out the corners. Insert the cardboard rectangle into the sleeve. Fold ¼" (6mm) of the felt

and fabric edges under, and hand stitch the opening closed (Fig. 5). Gently fold the case closed to crease the cardboard at the center fold.

**6** Optional: Embellish the inside of the case by hand stitching decorative felt flowers with E bead centers to one side of a needle strip.

Fig. 3

Fig. 4

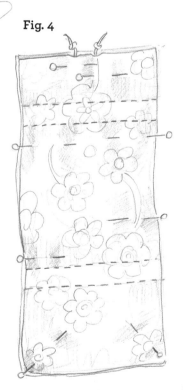

Fig. 5

# patterns

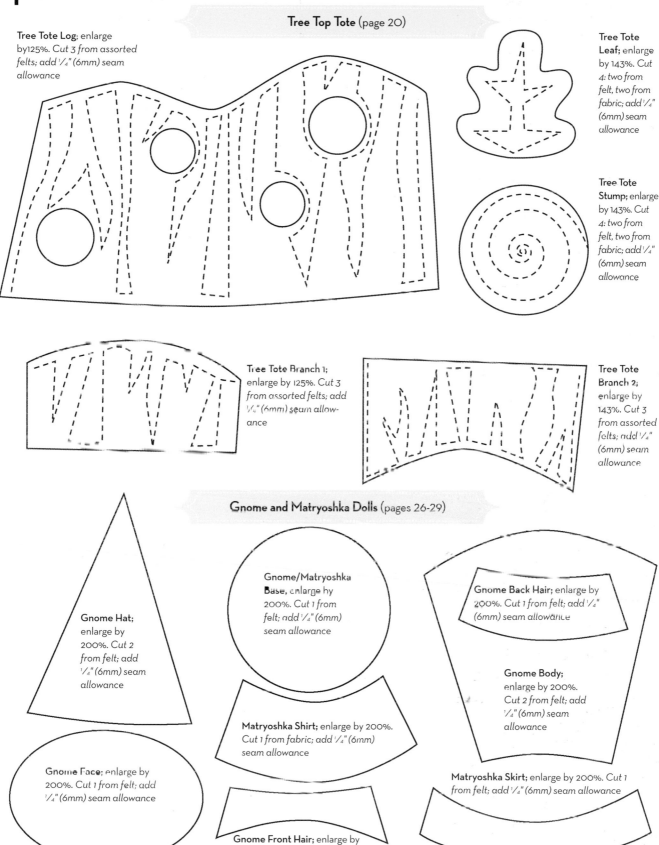

**Tree Top Tote** (page 20)

**Tree Tote Log;** enlarge by125%. Cut 3 from assorted felts; add ¼" (6mm) seam allowance

**Tree Tote Leaf;** enlarge by 143%. Cut 4: two from felt, two from fabric; add ¼" (6mm) seam allowance

**Tree Tote Stump;** enlarge by 143%. Cut 4: two from felt, two from fabric; add ¼" (6mm) seam allowance

**Tree Tote Branch 1;** enlarge by 125%. Cut 3 from assorted felts; add ¼" (6mm) seam allowance

**Tree Tote Branch 2;** enlarge by 143%. Cut 3 from assorted felts; add ¼" (6mm) seam allowance

**Gnome and Matryoshka Dolls** (pages 26-29)

**Gnome Hat;** enlarge by 200%. Cut 2 from felt; add ¼" (6mm) seam allowance

**Gnome/Matryoshka Base,** enlarge by 200%. Cut 1 from felt; add ¼" (6mm) seam allowance

**Gnome Back Hair;** enlarge by 200%. Cut 1 from felt; add ¼" (6mm) seam allowance

**Gnome Body;** enlarge by 200%. Cut 2 from felt; add ¼" (6mm) seam allowance

**Matryoshka Shirt;** enlarge by 200%. Cut 1 from fabric; add ¼" (6mm) seam allowance

**Gnome Face;** enlarge by 200%. Cut 1 from felt; add ¼" (6mm) seam allowance

**Matryoshka Skirt;** enlarge by 200%. Cut 1 from felt; add ¼" (6mm) seam allowance

**Gnome Front Hair;** enlarge by 200%. Cut 1 from felt; add ¼" (6mm) seam allowance

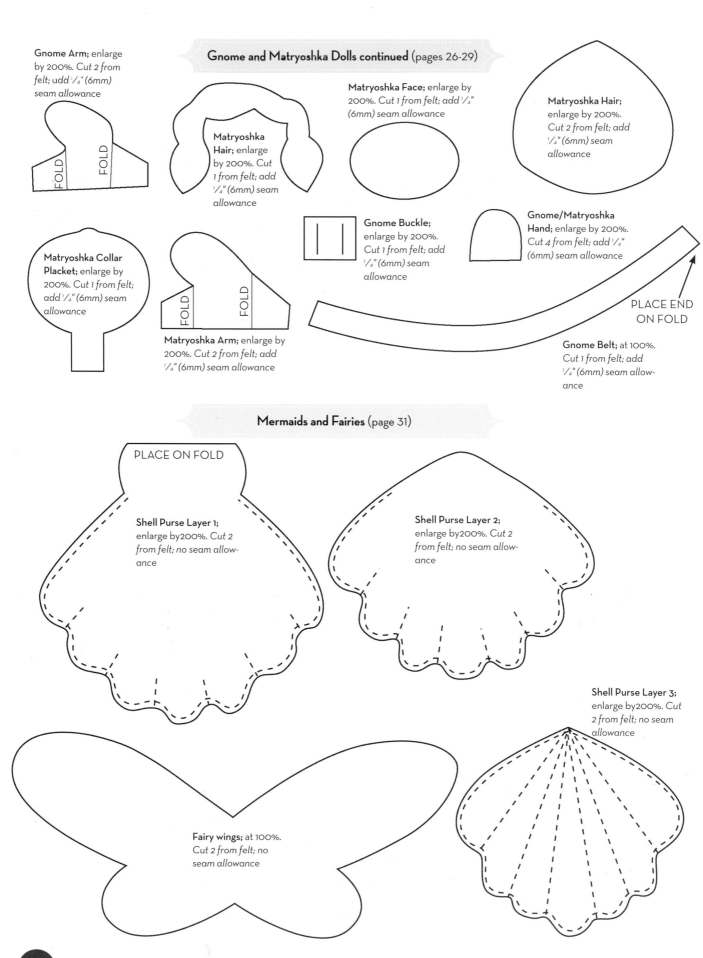

**Gnome Arm;** enlarge by 200%. Cut 2 from felt; add ¼" (6mm) seam allowance

FOLD  FOLD

**Gnome and Matryoshka Dolls continued** (pages 26-29)

**Matryoshka Hair;** enlarge by 200%. Cut 1 from felt; add ¼" (6mm) seam allowance

**Matryoshka Face;** enlarge by 200%. Cut 1 from felt; add ¼" (6mm) seam allowance

**Matryoshka Hair;** enlarge by 200%. Cut 2 from felt; add ¼" (6mm) seam allowance

**Matryoshka Collar Placket;** enlarge by 200%. Cut 1 from felt; add ¼" (6mm) seam allowance

**Matryoshka Arm;** enlarge by 200%. Cut 2 from felt; add ¼" (6mm) seam allowance

FOLD  FOLD

**Gnome Buckle;** enlarge by 200%. Cut 1 from felt; add ¼" (6mm) seam allowance

**Gnome/Matryoshka Hand;** enlarge by 200%. Cut 4 from felt; add ¼" (6mm) seam allowance

PLACE END ON FOLD

**Gnome Belt;** at 100%. Cut 1 from felt; add ¼" (6mm) seam allowance

**Mermaids and Fairies** (page 31)

PLACE ON FOLD

**Shell Purse Layer 1;** enlarge by 200%. Cut 2 from felt; no seam allowance

**Shell Purse Layer 2;** enlarge by 200%. Cut 2 from felt; no seam allowance

**Shell Purse Layer 3;** enlarge by 200%. Cut 2 from felt; no seam allowance

**Fairy wings;** at 100%. Cut 2 from felt; no seam allowance

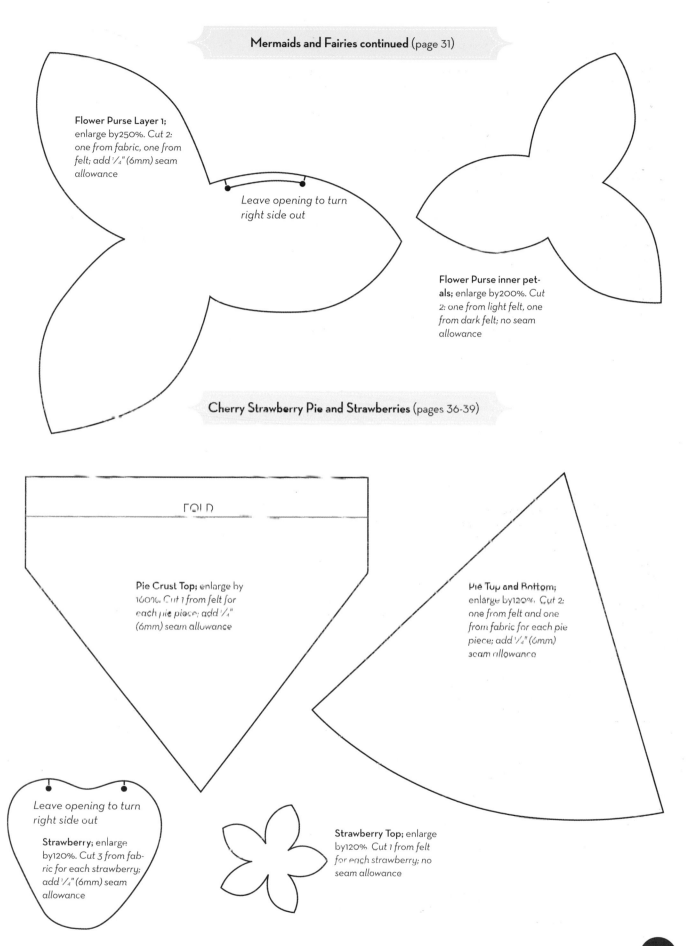

**Flower Purse Layer 1;** *enlarge by250%. Cut 2: one from fabric, one from felt; add ¼" (6mm) seam allowance*

*Leave opening to turn right side out*

**Flower Purse inner petals;** *enlarge by200%. Cut 2: one from light felt, one from dark felt; no seam allowance*

**Cherry Strawberry Pie and Strawberries** (pages 36-39)

FOLD

**Pie Crust Top;** *enlarge by 160%. Cut 1 from felt for each pie piece; add ¼" (6mm) seam allowance*

**Pie Top and Bottom;** *enlarge by120%. Cut 2: one from felt and one from fabric for each pie piece; add ¼" (6mm) seam allowance*

*Leave opening to turn right side out*

**Strawberry;** *enlarge by120%. Cut 3 from fabric for each strawberry; add ¼" (6mm) seam allowance*

**Strawberry Top;** *enlarge by120% Cut 1 from felt for each strawberry; no seam allowance*

**Back Crust;** enlarge by 120%. *Cut 1 from felt for each pie piece; add ¼" (6mm) seam allowance*

**Pie filling;** at 100%. Cut 1 from fabric for each pie piece; add ¼" (6mm) seam allowance

## Woodland Animal Ornaments (page 46)

FOLD

**Squirrel 4;** enlarge by 160%. *Cut 1 from felt; no seam allowance*

**Squirrel 5;** enlarge by 160%. *Cut 1 from felt; no seam allowance*

**Squirrel 7;** enlarge by 160%. *Cut 1 from felt; no seam allowance*

**Squirrel 3;** enlarge by 160%. *Cut 1 from felt; no seam allowance*

**Squirrel 6;** enlarge by 160%. *Cut 1 from felt; no seam allowance*

Squirrel 1; enlarge by 160%. *Cut 1 from felt; no seam allowance*

Squirrel 2; enlarge by 160%. *Cut 1 from felt; no seam allowance*

Rabbit 1; enlarge by 160%. *Cut 1 from felt; no seam allowance*

Rabbit 2; enlarge by 160%. *Cut 1 from felt; no seam allowance*

Rabbit 4; enlarge by 160%. *Cut 1 from felt; no allowance seam*

Rabbit 3; enlarge by 160%. *Cut 1 from felt; no seam allowance*

Rabbit 5; enlarge by 160%. *Cut 1 from medium felt; no seam allowance*

Rabbit 6; enlarge by 160%. *Cut 1 from felt; no seam allowance*

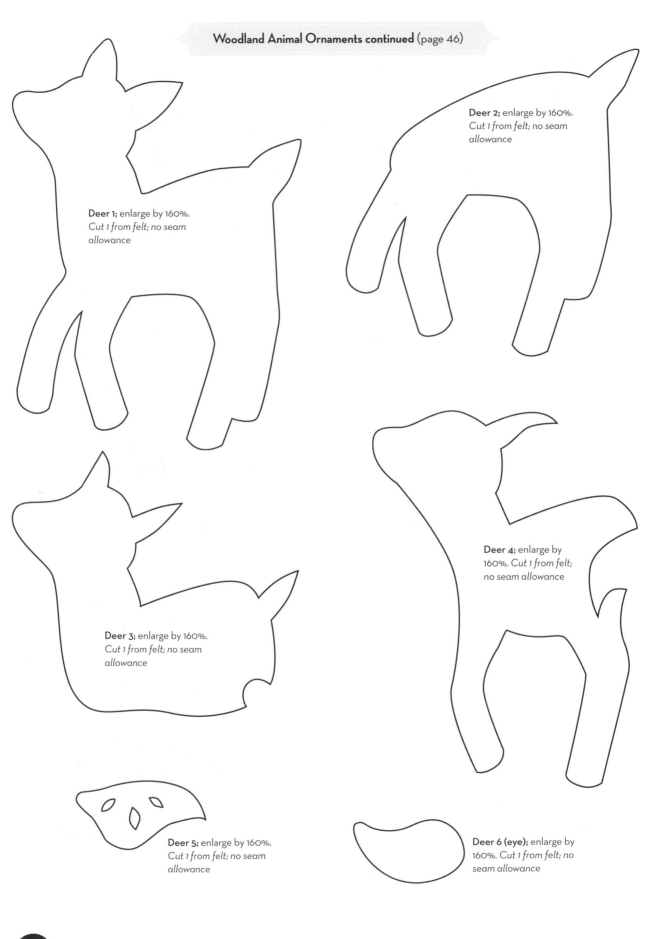

**Deer 1;** enlarge by 160%. *Cut 1 from felt; no seam allowance*

**Deer 2;** enlarge by 160%. *Cut 1 from felt; no seam allowance*

**Deer 3;** enlarge by 160%. *Cut 1 from felt; no seam allowance*

**Deer 4;** enlarge by 160%. *Cut 1 from felt; no seam allowance*

**Deer 5;** enlarge by 160%. *Cut 1 from felt; no seam allowance*

**Deer 6 (eye);** enlarge by 160%. *Cut 1 from felt; no seam allowance*

Fox 1; enlarge by 200%.
Cut 1 from felt; no seam
allowance

Fox 3; enlarge by 200%.
Cut 1 from light felt; no
seam allowance

Fox 2; enlarge by 200%.
Cut 1 from red felt; no
seam allowance

Fox 4; enlarge by 200%.
Cut 1 from red felt; no
seam allowance

Hedgehog 1; enlarge by
160%. Cut 1 from felt; no
seam allowance

Hedgehog 3; enlarge by
160%. Cut 1 from felt; no
seam allowance

Hedgehog 2; enlarge by
160%. Cut 1 from felt; no
seam allowance

Hedgehog 4; enlarge by
160%. Cut 1 from felt; no
seam allowance

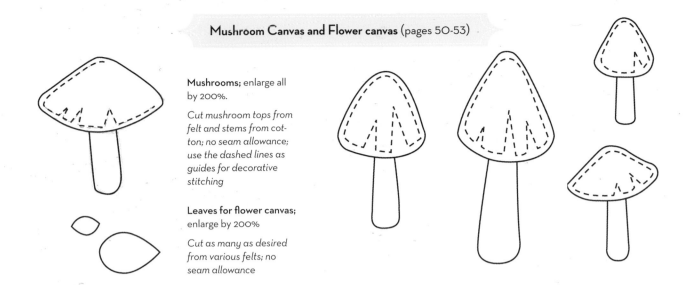

**Mushroom Canvas and Flower canvas** (pages 50-53)

**Mushrooms;** enlarge all by 200%.

*Cut mushroom tops from felt and stems from cotton; no seam allowance; use the dashed lines as guides for decorative stitching*

**Leaves for flower canvas;** enlarge by 200%

*Cut as many as desired from various felts; no seam allowance*

**Tabletop Trees** (page 54)

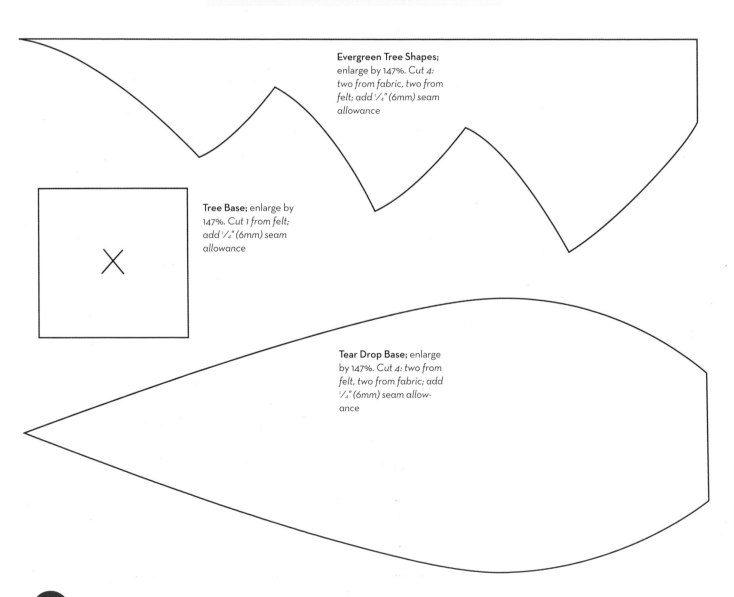

**Evergreen Tree Shapes;** enlarge by 147%. Cut 4: two from fabric, two from felt; add ¼" (6mm) seam allowance

**Tree Base;** enlarge by 147%. Cut 1 from felt; add ¼" (6mm) seam allowance

**Tear Drop Base;** enlarge by 147%. Cut 4: two from felt, two from fabric; add ¼" (6mm) seam allowance

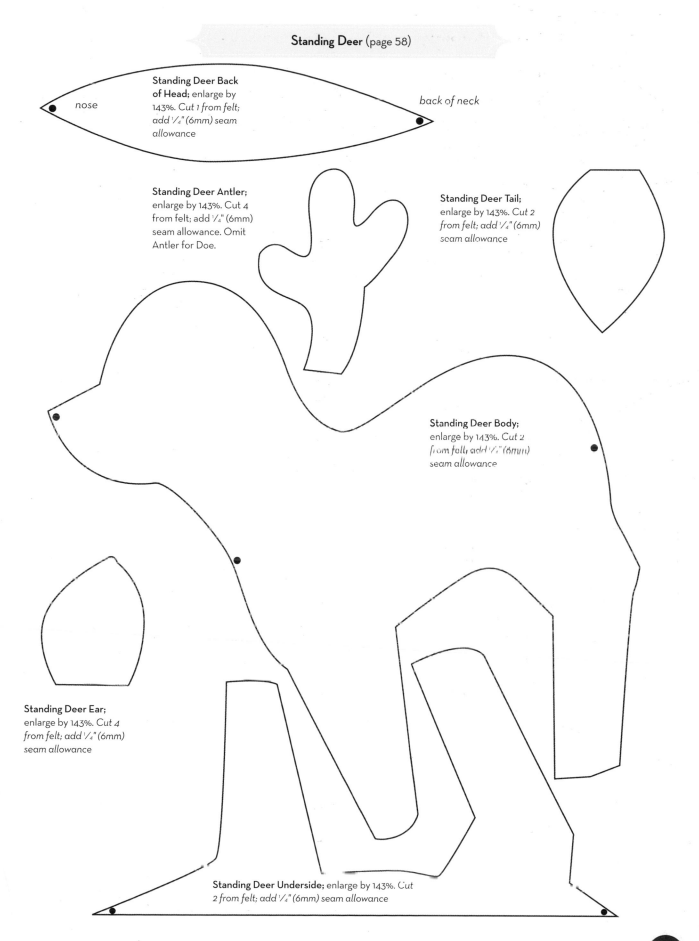

nose

**Standing Deer Back of Head;** enlarge by 143%. *Cut 1 from felt; add ¼" (6mm) seam allowance*

back of neck

**Standing Deer Antler;** enlarge by 143%. Cut 4 from felt; add ¼" (6mm) seam allowance. Omit Antler for Doe.

**Standing Deer Tail;** enlarge by 143%. *Cut 2 from felt; add ¼" (6mm) seam allowance*

**Standing Deer Body;** enlarge by 143%. *Cut 2 from felt; add ¼" (6mm) seam allowance*

**Standing Deer Ear;** enlarge by 143%. *Cut 4 from felt; add ¼" (6mm) seam allowance*

**Standing Deer Underside;** enlarge by 143%. *Cut 2 from felt; add ¼" (6mm) seam allowance*

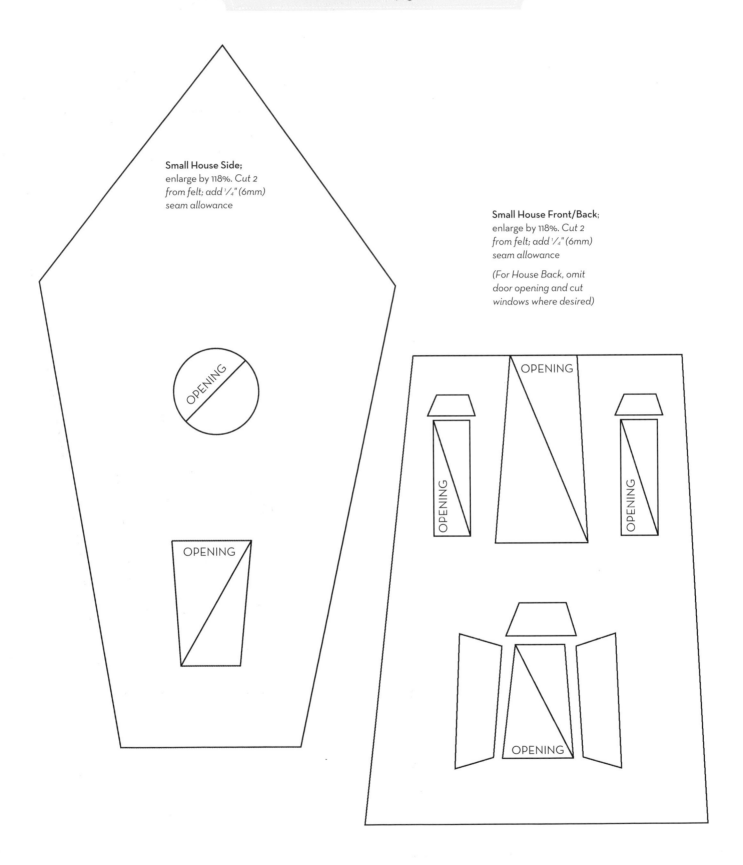

**Small House Side;**
enlarge by 118%. *Cut 2
from felt; add ¼" (6mm)
seam allowance*

**Small House Front/Back;**
enlarge by 118%. *Cut 2
from felt; add ¼" (6mm)
seam allowance*

*(For House Back, omit
door opening and cut
windows where desired)*

OPENING

OPENING

OPENING

OPENING

OPENING

OPENING

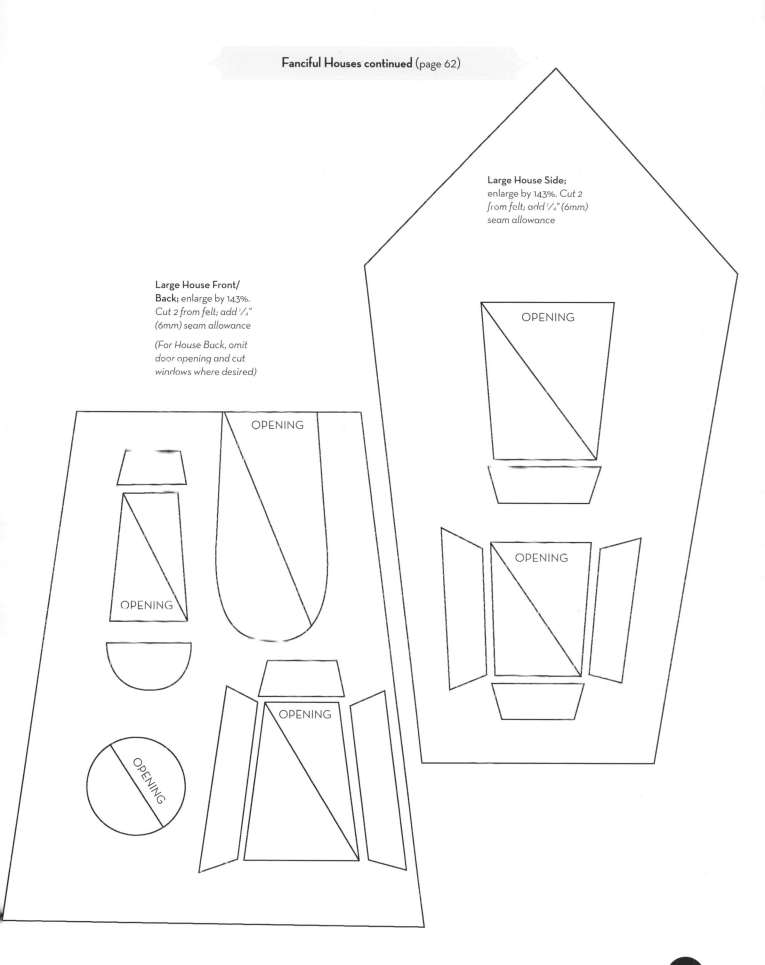

**Large House Side;** enlarge by 143%. *Cut 2 from felt; add ¼" (6mm) seam allowance*

OPENING

OPENING

**Large House Front/ Back;** enlarge by 143%. *Cut 2 from felt; add ¼" (6mm) seam allowance*

*(For House Back, omit door opening and cut windows where desired)*

OPENING

OPENING

OPENING

OPENING

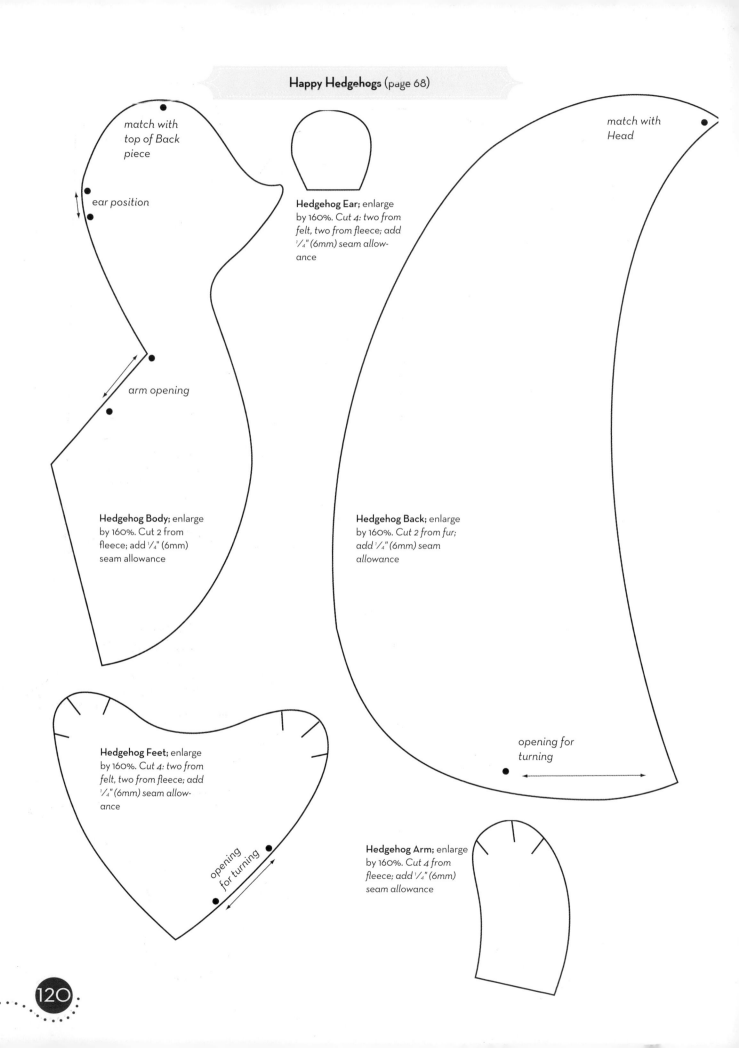

match with top of Back piece

ear position

arm opening

Hedgehog Ear; enlarge by 160%. Cut 4: two from felt, two from fleece; add ¼" (6mm) seam allowance

match with Head

Hedgehog Body; enlarge by 160%. Cut 2 from fleece; add ¼" (6mm) seam allowance

Hedgehog Back; enlarge by 160%. Cut 2 from fur; add ¼" (6mm) seam allowance

opening for turning

Hedgehog Feet; enlarge by 160%. Cut 4: two from felt, two from fleece; add ¼" (6mm) seam allowance

opening for turning

Hedgehog Arm; enlarge by 160%. Cut 4 from fleece; add ¼" (6mm) seam allowance

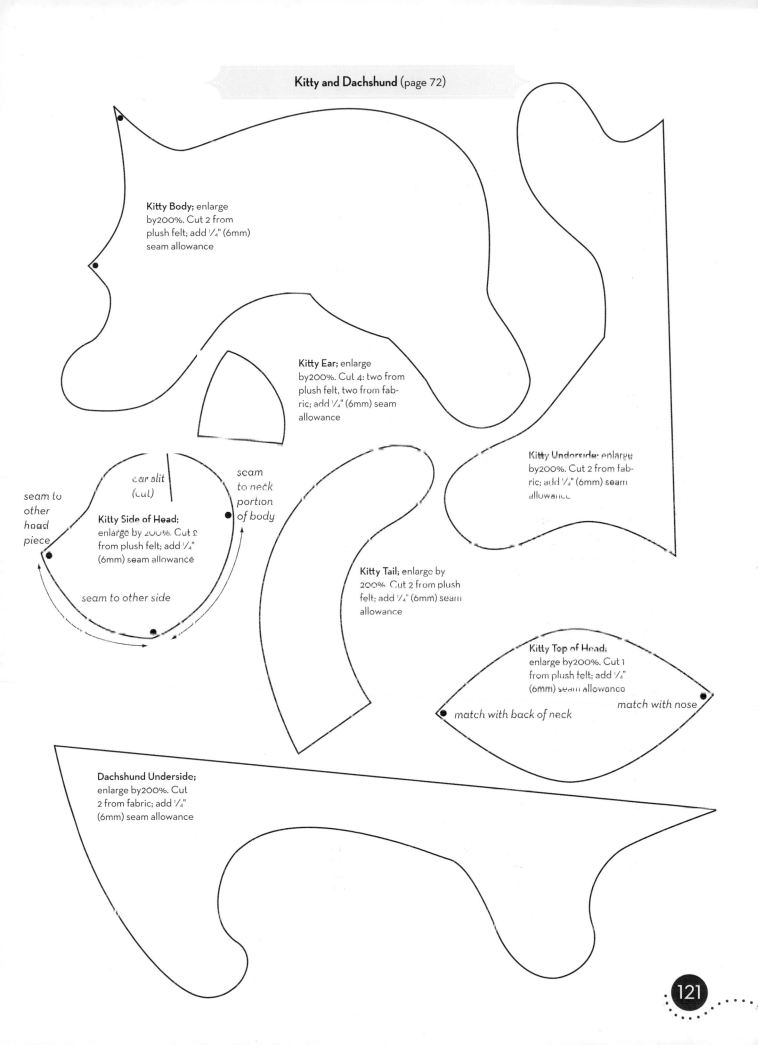

**Kitty Body;** enlarge by200%. Cut 2 from plush felt; add ¼" (6mm) seam allowance

**Kitty Ear;** enlarge by200%. Cut 4: two from plush felt, two from fabric; add ¼" (6mm) seam allowance

**Kitty Underside;** enlarge by200%. Cut 2 from fabric; add ¼" (6mm) seam allowance

*seam to other head piece*

*ear slit (cut)*

*seam to neck portion of body*

**Kitty Side of Head;** enlarge by 200%. Cut 2 from plush felt; add ¼" (6mm) seam allowance

*seam to other side*

**Kitty Tail;** enlarge by 200%. Cut 2 from plush felt; add ¼" (6mm) seam allowance

**Kitty Top of Head;** enlarge by200%. Cut 1 from plush felt; add ¼" (6mm) seam allowance

*match with back of neck*

*match with nose*

**Dachshund Underside;** enlarge by200%. Cut 2 from fabric; add ¼" (6mm) seam allowance

*ear position*

**Dachshund Body;**
*enlarge by200%. Cut 2
from plush felt; add ¼"
(6mm) seam allowance*

**Dachshund Ear;** *enlarge
by200%. Cut 4: two from
fabric, two from plush
felt; add ¼" (6mm) seam
allowance*

**Dachshund Tail;** *enlarge
by200%. Cut 2 from
plush felt; add ¼" (6mm)
seam allowance*

*nose end*

**Dachshund Top of Head;**
*enlarge by200%. Cut 1
from plush felt; add ¼"
(6mm) seam allowance*

*back of neck*

**Snappy Turtle** (page 76)

**Turtle Shell Rim;** *enlarge
by200%. Cut 2 from fab-
ric; add ¼" (6mm) seam
allowance*

*connect to neck*

**Turtle Shell Top;** *enlarge
by200%. Cut 2 from fleece;
add ¼" (6mm) seam allow-
ance*

**Turtle head;** *enlarge
by200%. Cut 2 from
fleece; add ¼" (6mm)
seam allowance*

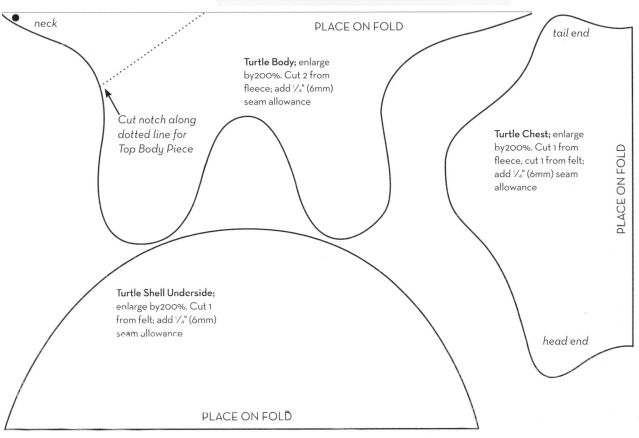

neck

PLACE ON FOLD

tail end

**Turtle Body;** enlarge by200%. Cut 2 from fleece; add ¼" (6mm) seam allowance

*Cut notch along dotted line for Top Body Piece*

**Turtle Chest;** enlarge by200%. Cut 1 from fleece, cut 1 from felt; add ¼" (6mm) seam allowance

PLACE ON FOLD

**Turtle Shell Underside;** enlarge by200%. Cut 1 from felt; add ¼" (6mm) seam allowance

head end

PLACE ON FOLD

## Summer Friends (page 80)

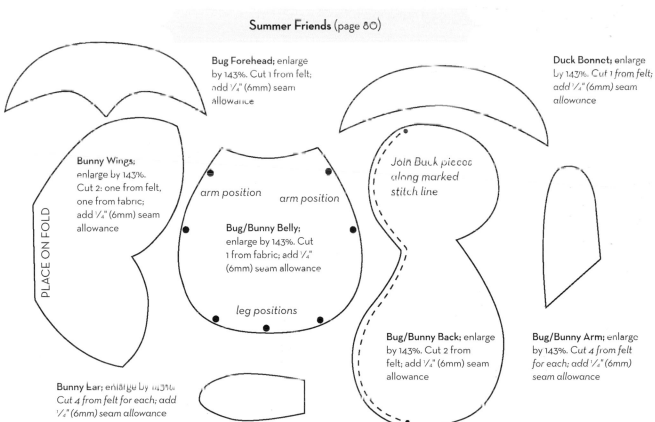

**Bug Forehead;** enlarge by 143%. Cut 1 from felt; add ¼" (6mm) seam allowance

**Duck Bonnet;** enlarge by 143%. Cut 1 from felt; add ¼" (6mm) seam allowance

**Bunny Wings;** enlarge by 143%. Cut 2: one from felt, one from tabric; add ¼" (6mm) seam allowance

arm position    arm position

*Join Back pieces along marked stitch line*

PLACE ON FOLD

**Bug/Bunny Belly;** enlarge by 143%. Cut 1 from fabric; add ¼" (6mm) seam allowance

leg positions

**Bug/Bunny Back;** enlarge by 143%. Cut 2 from felt; add ¼" (6mm) seam allowance

**Bug/Bunny Arm;** enlarge by 143%. Cut 4 from felt for each; add ¼" (6mm) seam allowance

**Bunny Ear;** enlarge by 143%. Cut 4 from felt for each; add ¼" (6mm) seam allowance

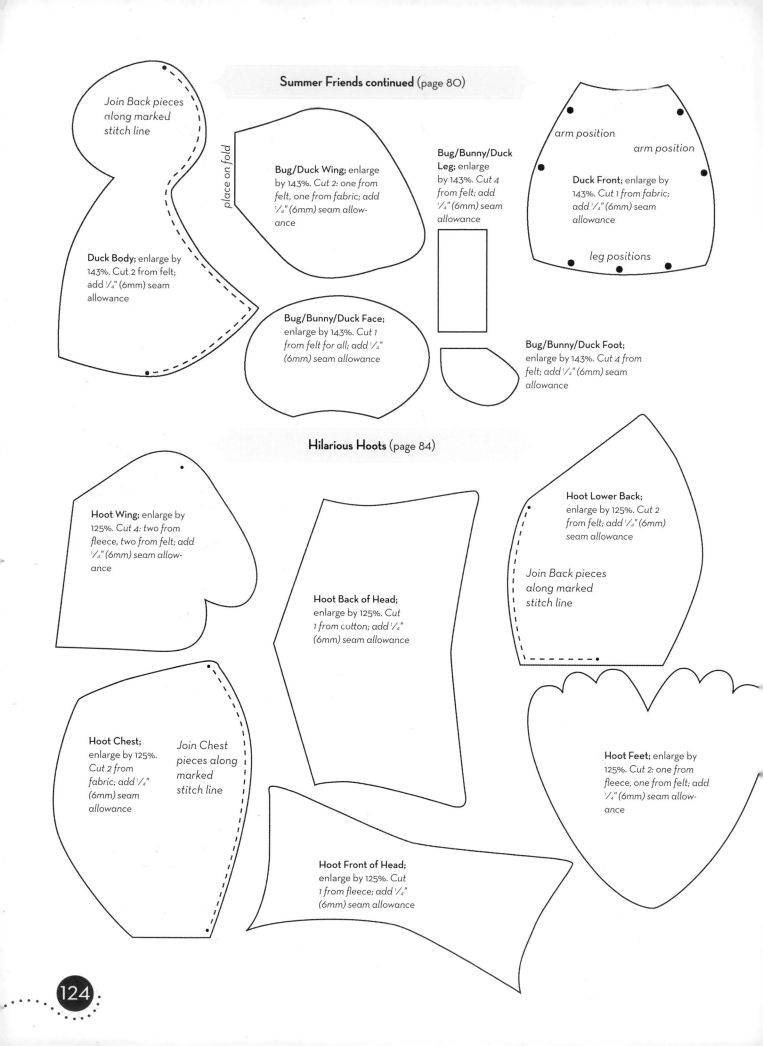

*Join Back pieces along marked stitch line*

*place on fold*

Bug/Duck Wing; enlarge by 143%. Cut 2: one from felt, one from fabric; add ¼" (6mm) seam allowance

Bug/Bunny/Duck Leg; enlarge by 143%. Cut 4 from felt; add ¼" (6mm) seam allowance

arm position

arm position

Duck Front; enlarge by 143%. Cut 1 from fabric; add ¼" (6mm) seam allowance

leg positions

Duck Body; enlarge by 143%. Cut 2 from felt; add ¼" (6mm) seam allowance

Bug/Bunny/Duck Face; enlarge by 143%. Cut 1 from felt for all; add ¼" (6mm) seam allowance

Bug/Bunny/Duck Foot; enlarge by 143%. Cut 4 from felt; add ¼" (6mm) seam allowance

## Hilarious Hoots (page 84)

Hoot Wing; enlarge by 125%. Cut 4: two from fleece, two from felt; add ¼" (6mm) seam allowance

Hoot Lower Back; enlarge by 125%. Cut 2 from felt; add ¼" (6mm) seam allowance

*Join Back pieces along marked stitch line*

Hoot Back of Head; enlarge by 125%. Cut 1 from cotton; add ¼" (6mm) seam allowance

Hoot Chest; enlarge by 125%. Cut 2 from fabric; add ¼" (6mm) seam allowance

*Join Chest pieces along marked stitch line*

Hoot Feet; enlarge by 125%. Cut 2: one from fleece, one from felt; add ¼" (6mm) seam allowance

Hoot Front of Head; enlarge by 125%. Cut 1 from fleece; add ¼" (6mm) seam allowance

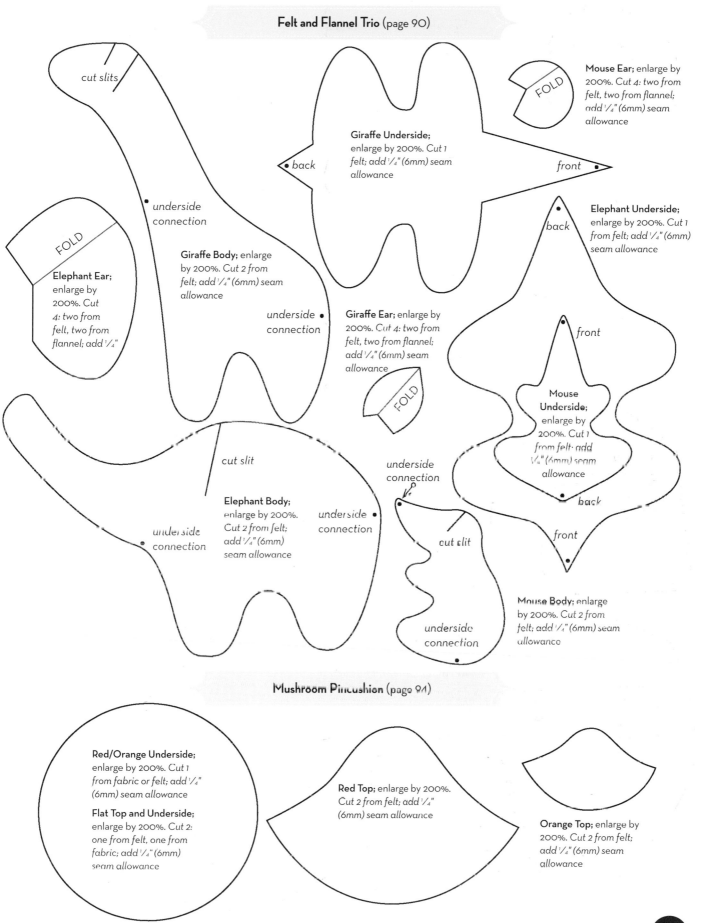

**Felt and Flannel Trio** (page 90)

cut slits

Mouse Ear; enlarge by 200%. Cut 4: two from felt, two from flannel; add 1/4" (6mm) seam allowance

FOLD

Giraffe Underside; enlarge by 200%. Cut 1 felt; add 1/4" (6mm) seam allowance

• back

front •

• underside connection

Elephant Underside; enlarge by 200%. Cut 1 from felt; add 1/4" (6mm) seam allowance

• back

FOLD

Elephant Ear; enlarge by 200%. Cut 4: two from felt, two from flannel; add 1/4"

Giraffe Body; enlarge by 200%. Cut 2 from felt; add 1/4" (6mm) seam allowance

• underside connection

front •

Giraffe Ear; enlarge by 200%. Cut 4: two from felt, two from flannel; add 1/4" (6mm) seam allowance

FOLD

Mouse Underside; enlarge by 200%. Cut 1 from felt; add 1/4" (6mm) seam allowance

cut slit

underside connection

• back

• underside connection

front •

Elephant Body; enlarge by 200%. Cut 2 from felt; add 1/4" (6mm) seam allowance

• underside connection

cut slit

• underside connection

Mouse Body; enlarge by 200%. Cut 2 from felt; add 1/4" (6mm) seam allowance

• underside connection

**Mushroom Pincushion** (page 91)

Red/Orange Underside; enlarge by 200%. Cut 1 from fabric or felt; add 1/4" (6mm) seam allowance

Flat Top and Underside; enlarge by 200%. Cut 2: one from felt, one from fabric; add 1/4" (6mm) seam allowance

Red Top; enlarge by 200%. Cut 2 from felt; add 1/4" (6mm) seam allowance

Orange Top; enlarge by 200%. Cut 2 from felt; add 1/4" (6mm) seam allowance

# Birds in a Nest (page 98)

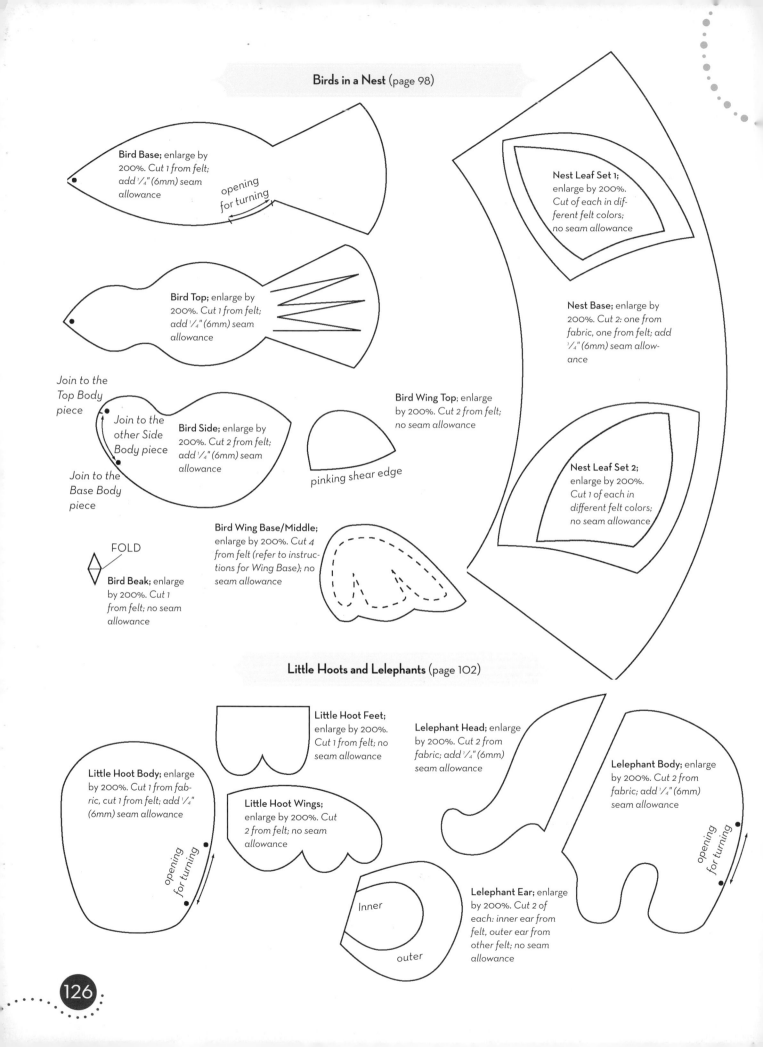

Bird Base; enlarge by 200%. Cut 1 from felt; add 1/4" (6mm) seam allowance

opening for turning

Bird Top; enlarge by 200%. Cut 1 from felt; add 1/4" (6mm) seam allowance

Join to the Top Body piece

Join to the other Side Body piece

Join to the Base Body piece

Bird Side; enlarge by 200%. Cut 2 from felt; add 1/4" (6mm) seam allowance

Bird Wing Top; enlarge by 200%. Cut 2 from felt; no seam allowance

pinking shear edge

Nest Leaf Set 1; enlarge by 200%. Cut of each in different felt colors; no seam allowance

Nest Base; enlarge by 200%. Cut 2: one from fabric, one from felt; add 1/4" (6mm) seam allowance

Nest Leaf Set 2; enlarge by 200%. Cut 1 of each in different felt colors; no seam allowance

FOLD

Bird Beak; enlarge by 200%. Cut 1 from felt; no seam allowance

Bird Wing Base/Middle; enlarge by 200%. Cut 4 from felt (refer to instructions for Wing Base); no seam allowance

## Little Hoots and Lelephants (page 102)

Little Hoot Feet; enlarge by 200%. Cut 1 from felt; no seam allowance

Lelephant Head; enlarge by 200%. Cut 2 from fabric; add 1/4" (6mm) seam allowance

Lelephant Body; enlarge by 200%. Cut 2 from fabric; add 1/4" (6mm) seam allowance

Little Hoot Body; enlarge by 200%. Cut 1 from fabric, cut 1 from felt; add 1/4" (6mm) seam allowance

opening for turning

Little Hoot Wings; enlarge by 200%. Cut 2 from felt; no seam allowance

Inner

outer

Lelephant Ear; enlarge by 200%. Cut 2 of each: inner ear from felt, outer ear from other felt; no seam allowance

opening for turning

# index

# Sew Cute!

## Sweet Needle Felts

### 25 Projects to Wear, Give & Hug

*By Jenn Docherty*

Sweet Needle Felts features all the techniques and information you need to begin needle felting. Included are 25 whimsical projects featuring wearable items such as hats, scarves and jewelry along with home décor, dolls and toys like the quick-to-make Woolly Critter T. Striking, colorful wool gives each project a bright and cheery look that is guaranteed to inspire gifts for dear friends or special treats for yourself.

## Warm Fuzzies

### 30 Sweet Felted Projects

*By Betz White*

Create 30 cute and colorful felted projects, including cozy pillows and throws as well as comfortable hats, scarves, pincushions and handbags. Betz White shows you how to felt bargain sweaters, then use them to make quick, adorable projects for the whole family. Learn how to select the best wool for felting, the best way to full it, and combine this process with a variety of techniques, including appliqué, knitted I-cord, embroidery, needle felting and more.

Learn more about needlecrafts with these and other fine sewing and needle felting titles available at your local craft retailer, bookstore or online supplier.